THE ENCYCLOPEDIA OF WEALTH BUILDING FINANCIAL OPPORTUNITIES

MONEY MANUAL NO. 1—PLANT YOUR DOLLARS IN REAL ESTATE AND WATCH THEM GROW
The Basics Of Real Estate Investing

MONEY MANUAL NO. 2—INVESTMENT OPPORTUNITIES OF THE 1980'S
Wealth Building Strategies In The Stock Market, Gold, Silver, Diamonds...

MONEY MANUAL NO. 3—SECRETS OF THE MILLIONAIRES
How The Rich Made It Big

MONEY MANUAL NO. 4—DYNAMICS OF PERSONAL MONEY MANAGEMENT
How To Save, Manage, And Multiply Your Money

MONEY MANUAL NO. 5—THE NEW AGE OF BANKING
Secrets Of Banking And Borrowing

MONEY MANUAL NO. 6—HOW TO START MAKING MONEY IN A BUSINESS OF YOUR OWN
A Guide To Money Making Opportunities

MONEY MANUAL NO. 7—HOW TO SAVE ON TAXES AND TAKE ALL THE DEDUCTIONS YOU ARE ENTITLED TO

DYNAMICS
OF
PERSONAL MONEY
MANAGEMENT

How To Save, Manage and Multiply Your Money

Published by:

George Sterne
Profit Ideas
8361 Vickers St., Suite 304
San Diego, California 92111

ACKNOWLEDGEMENTS

The publishers wish to express thanks to John Oesterle for his contribution of research and writing to this book.

Library of Congress Catalog Card Number 78-64391
ISBN 0-940398-03-6

CONTENTS

FOREWORD

You are the consumer, the moneymaker who makes up the American market. Your decisions on what to buy determine what the industry of this country will produce. After all if nobody will buy a product then the company that makes the product will not produce any more of that product. Conversely, if you patronize a product or a company that sells a good product that company will prosper and you will benefit from the support given to a good company.

No matter what your income you will without a doubt benefit from reading this book. Being aware of the opportunities that are available for increasing your quality of life makes it easy to take advantage of the best deals. Most people really do not know how to go about the best way of making a major purchase or investment. You will find fairly complete chapters on these topics.

This volume contains the essentials of shopping strategy. A shopping strategy does not mean taking enough cash to the store when you are shopping. It means carefully planning your shopping. Major expenditures should be researched. You should become an expert on where the bargains are. That goes for everyday purchases as well as major purchases and investments.

The book should be read through once to get an idea of the magnitude of the money management concept. Then, as individual money decisions come up, you can refer to the chapters to refresh your memory. This will also give you an opportunity to reevaluate your strategy.

I urge you to take the time to become a good manager of your money. It definitely pays off - in dollars as well as personal satisfaction. Why work so hard at making money when with the expertise you will find in this book you can get so much more. Give yourself a raise, be a good personal money manager.

Chapter One

BUDGETING - THE PLAN

People have more money than ever to spend today. Getting the most for your money involves setting up a plan for your money. The plan involves viewing your household budget as your personal enterprise. Every business uses a financial plan and so should you. Of course, everyone's plan will be different as all people are different and as all people have different desires. Understanding and relating your desires to a plan to achieve your goals is the most important step you can take towards a rewarding financial plan.

If you do not have a plan you may suffer. Money problems are one of the leading sources of marital discord. If you are spending your paycheck without a plan, then it will - unless you have a very large paycheck - be hard for you to achieve financial goals that will provide the things you wanted but thought you could not afford. A budget will get you many things you may have thought were impossible to get. It should also tell you what is not possible. In any event it is only fair to yourself to take the time to plan out what you would like to do with your money.

What a Budget Can Do For You

I have a friend who has for as long as I can remember

always wanted a yacht. Well, a couple of months ago he went out and bought a 42 foot hull, brand new, highest quality, and completely stripped down. This boat does not even have a steering wheel on it. It cost him $39,000 and he plans to outfit it at a cost of $20,000 in five years. The completed boat today sells for around $100,000 depending on the amount and quality of electronic gear desired. Now you ask, how much does he have to make to able to afford a $100,000 yacht? Well, he makes $15,000 a year, supports a beautiful wife and has a very nice apartment.

Very soon I'm afraid he will have to answer a question he should have asked himself before he bought his yacht: Where is he going to get the money ($20,000) to outift this fantastic hull? The answer is that there is no foreseeable place that he can pick up the cash to complete his project. If he manages to get it in the water and tries to save rent money by living aboard ship he will have another big problem - the interior has not been completed and even if he did manage to complete the interior the quarters might be slightly close over five years.

If my friend had seriously budgeted his money for the project he might have had a slight disappointment but I'm sure it would have been considerably less than what he is now facing.

A budget would have shown him what kind of a boat he could afford.

How to Make a Budget that will Work

The Plan-

A budget is a plan for spending and earning your money. It requires that you sit down or pace if you prefer and come up with a set of financial goals Some goals might be:

Owning my own house.

Spending several weeks traveling on vacation every year in Europe.

Having a retirement income that will allow me great freedom.

Owning a resort cottage.

Having a secure job that I enjoy.

Supporting a family in the manner that I would prefer to become accustomed to.

Whatever your goals may be, it will be much easier to attain them if you will make yourself a plan that identifies what you want and how you can get it. I have provided a form to help you write down your desires regarding financial achievements. Be sure to take time to think your goals through in a realistic manner. If you have problems about knowing what each goal will cost, get in touch with an expert in that particular field and/or read a book about it. There are numerous sources of literature about all the goals I mentioned above. The library contains books and current periodicals describing what is available to the consumer and at what expense. Do take the time to investigate. You will thank yourself later when you have attained your goal.

Chart of Goals

Lifetime goals:

Goals within five years from today:

Goals within one year from today:

Monthly goals:

Don't forget you can attain your goals more than once. Many people feel that a goal is a one shot deal but this is not so. In soccer, football, baseball or most any game scoring points or goals is a repetitive process. The more goals you score the more of a success you will be. Also do not be afraid to change your goal or even eliminate a goal. You win some and you lose some and some go into overtime.

As you begin your plan you will no doubt realize that it is very difficult to plan precisely what you will achieve. This is not the idea of the plan. For instance if you plan to own your home and your plan calls for a 4 bedroom, 2 and one-half bath, English Tudor style home on a two and one-half acre estate overlooking a picturesque rural valley, but while looking for this elusive creature you come across a ranch style home of an equivalent nature that you fall in love with, well, then, take it. You see, the goal was to acquire a beautiful home that you could enjoy living in and you have found it.

Planning for Income

	Jan.	Feb.	Mar.	Apr.	May	June	July	Aug.	Sept.	Oct.	Nov.	Dec.	TOTALS
Husband's income (net)													
Wife's income (net)													
Dividends													
Interest													
Profit from sales													
Rental (net) income													
Bonuses													
Alimony													
Child Support													
Other													
TOTALS													

The next step after deciding what your goals are, is to list your expected sources of income for the next year. Most of you will have to make a new chart each year to accomodate new sources of income. The chart should show your income net of all payroll deductions. Rental income should be shown net of mortgage, taxes, insurance, and maintenance.

The figures used in this chart should be exact. Once you know what you have to spend, it will be easy to know what you can spend and what you can save and invest. The income chart used in conjunction with the spending chart will greatly enlighten you as to what you can really do with the money you earn.

Spending Money

The average American's spending habits for the mid-seventies are shown below:

	Percent spent after taxes
Food, alcohol and tobacco	22.3%
Housing	14.5%
Household expenses	14.4%
Transportation	13.6%
Clothing	10.1%
Medical	7.7%
Recreation	6.5%
Personal business	5.6%
Education	1.7%
Personal care	1.5%
Religious and civic activities	1.4%
Foreign travel	.7%

I doubt very much that your spending will look very much like the above except that the top 4 or 5 items will probably remain at the top of the list. Also not shown on the list is savings; one of the most important components of your budget. As you will see later on in the chapter the key to financial security for most of us is the ability to set aside money for future use.

After you have determined how much money you have to spend, you will want to set up a method for spending it in a rational manner. Your plan will be as comprehensive as possible since if you forget items that you will be spending on, the budget may not be able to absorb these things. So the first step is to make a list of items that you spend money on. The list should begin with the basic expenses of living that are necessary. Missing a payment on these expenses may create problems:

	Jan.	Feb.	Mar.	Apr.	May	June	July	Aug.	Sept.	Oct.	Nov.	Dec.	TOTALS
Rent or Mortgage payment													
Utilities: Gas													
Electric													
Fuel													
Water													
Phone													
Charge Accounts													
Loans: Personal													
Home Improve.													
Auto													
Education													
Insurance Homeowners or Apt.													
Health													
Life													
Auto													
Medical & Dental													
Savings & Investments													
Taxes Property tax if not in monthly mortgate payment													
Income tax due or refund.													
Goals: Monthly													
5 Years													
Lifetime													
TOTAL													

The above list should then be estimated for each month, similar to the income chart. Figure out what your payments will be for each month in each of the categories. Medical and dental should be an average of the past few year's bills with 10% to 15% more for inflation or extra visits. If your property taxes are due in one large payment at the beginning of your budget or before you have accumulated enough money from monthly allocations to cover the amount due, then simply draw into your savings for the amount and **don't** forget to replace the withdrawal with monthly allocations to the savings account to repay the account and remember that the next lump sum due should be set aside in advance rather than interrupting the savings account.

Adjustable expenses include allowances for the following:

	Jan.	Feb.	Mar.	Apr.	May	June	July	Aug.	Sept.	Oct.	Nov.	Dec.	TOTALS
Food: At home													
Restaurants													
Clothing: Husband													
Wife													
Children													
Transportation: Gas													
Maintenance													
Furniture													
Education													
Vacations													
Holidays													
Gifts													
Allowances: Husband													
Wife													
Children													
Miscellaneous: Maintenance													
Cleaning													
Repairs and Replacements													
Other:													
Contributions													
Total Adjustable Expenses													

In brief form this is what has been accomplished so far:

1. Establishment of a set of goals

2. Determination of near term income.

3. Determination of basic near term expenses

4. Determination of adjustable near term expenses

The next step is to subtract #3 and #4 from #2 to determine what is left to carryover to the next month. If you find that there is no carryover, then you will have to make an adjustment in the budget. The quickest cutbacks are in the adjustable expense. If you find a large carryover at the end of the year, then, you probably forgot something.

It is important to remember that the basic expenses can be adjusted also, and the greatest savings may be possible in this area, however it usually takes longer to make adjustments in the area of basic expenses.

	Jan.	Feb.	Mar.	Apr.	May	June	July	Aug.	Sept.	Oct.	Nov.	Dec.	TOTALS
INCOME Use Average Per Month													
Carryover Plus or Minus													
Minus Basic Expenses													
Minus Adjustable Expenses													
Equals Carryover													

Just by filling out the above, you will be able to see easily where you spend your money and if there may be areas where improvement may be easily accomplished. Of course, if you know that you are financially secure in the future then you may not have to adjust your spending. However, if you can see at this point that you may not have enough to reach your goals under the current budget then you must answer the question of whether the goals you want are worth the adjustment in the budget.

Time

To really do a budget that will work, you must take time. Time is needed to contemplate your goals and their desireability to you. In addition, time is needed to explore what these goals will cost and what methods of purchasing are available to you. This book will give you guidelines to explore the possibility of attaining each goal.

One other word about time; time is your most valuable asset. It is a flexible framework from within which we work, play, and sleep. Do not plan so rigidly that you cannot make adjustments for new interests or developments in your life.

Put Someone in Charge

If you are a single household, you are automatically nominated for the job. If there are two or more of you, then you can either alternate or pick someone who has the time and inclination to work the plan every month. A convenient time might be when you get your monthly checking statement. It's really very simple to do, you can even do it while watching T.V.

Bank Accounts

Theoretically, you could have one bank account for each section of your budget; one for utilities, one for savings, etc. However, the expense of checking accounts from one to three dollars a month makes this fairly uneconomical. The opposite extreme and cheapest way to go is with one checking account. If you are a couple and each have a personal checking account and a joint account it may be costing you close to $50 a year. Why not have one joint account at $12 a year and save $38.

Put your savings in savings accounts and your spending money in a checking account. Keep track of what is spent by the record in your check book or by the cancelled checks.

Emergency Fund

Your emergency fund is the first target of your savings. The fund should equal three to six months net income after deductions, or more, depending on the nature of your work and the amount of your basic expenses. (see page 8) If your basic expenses are low, then the emergency fund can be lower, but if you have a large mortgage payment and other debts you should try as much as possible for a strong six month fund. Keep this fund in a long term interest account unless you expect to be using it. You should not be using this fund for balancing out seasonal income. It is only for the unexpected necessities. Hence, emergency fund.

Tax Records

Records are a necessary item required by law. Stop by your local income tax preparation service office or your accountant's and pick up a folder or list of the types of records you should keep. Also see chapter seven in this book for a set of guidelines and a list of items you should keep to fulfill your legal obligations.

Other

Do not OTHER your budget to death. Try to think of and itemize as many other expenses as you might come up with. Then allow 2 to 5% of your income for this unexpected expense. If you don't spend your other, then you can include it in your savings and reach your goals that much quicker.

NOTES

26

Chapter Two

BUYING - THE BARGAINS
AND THE RIP-OFFS

There is hardly an item or a service available today that you cannot be taken on. The following list of the top twenty complaints received at the United States Office of Consumer Affairs points out the fact that even products or services considered to be reputable are vulnerable to complaints by the consumer.

Consumer Complaints

1974	1975	1976
Autos	Autos	Autos
Mail order	Mail order	Mail order
Credit	Housing	Business
Appliances	Packaging	Appliances
Business	Appliances	Credit
Housing	Business	Housing
Food	Credit	Insurance
Travel	Food	Advertising
Prices	Prices	Travel
Advertising	Insurance	Periodicals
TV/Radio	Travel	TV/Radio
Insurance	TV/Radio	Prices
Energy	Ads	Tires
Periodical	Furniture	Furniture

Movers	Utilities	Utilities
Furniture	Periodicals	Mobile homes
Household items	Household items	Healthcare
Books	Mobile Homes	Household items
Mobile homes	Movers	Home repair
Home repair	Home repair	

The Council of Better Business Bureaus reports the ratio of complaints settled to complaints received.

Lowest Percent of Complaints Settled

Legal services	Waterproofing Companies
Reupholstering	Auto Repair-Except transmission
Business opportunities	Market Research
Work at home opportunities	Home Remodeling
Vacation certificates	Automotive
Paving contractors	Service stations
Miscellaneous Home repair	Hair Products

This list does not indicate that these industries had or did not have many complaints, only that of the complaints officially received, many were not resolved by the Bette. Business Bureaus.

General Rules for Shopping

The best way to avoid having to make a complaint is to shop with care. Getting the most real value for your dollar means being familiar with the several principles that the well-advised shopper uses when shopping.

Decision to Buy

The decision to buy should come from within. Don't be talked into something that you will regret later. The item or service must fit some physical or psychological need **and** your budget. As emotional as advertising tends to make buying, the best shoppers make cold, calculated decisions and then enjoy the benefits of the purchase.

Evaluations of the Buy

Once you have decided that you are going to buy, you should learn what you can about the potential purchases. Of course, you will find that for smaller purchases you will not spend much time in the evaluation of which brand to buy. It simply is not worth the time and effort to spend hours shopping for a two dollar purchase. The best means of evaluation are listed below:

1. SHOPPING - as stores and brands as you have time for.

2. CONSUMER MAGAZINES - will prepare you for what you see on the shelf.

3. FRIENDS' ADVICE - the more people you poll about a

particular purchase the better your chances of getting reliable information. Not all people will be good shoppers as you will see.

The Other Considerations

1. Who the seller is - does he stand behind his product

2. Time of year - chart below shows the best times of year for purchases

3. Sales - be careful that it is on your list, some stores are **always** having sales. If you have really shopped around you should know a true sale and value.

4. Convenience stores - are expensive because they charge for convenience

5. List - use a list of the items you are ready to purchase.

6. Cash - use cash money; doesn't earn interest in your checking account and cash avoids overextension of credit and the budget.

7. Credit - only when convenience dictates

8. Checks - if you are afraid to carry too much cash for a large purchase.

9. Quality - good equals poor quality; better equals good quality; best equals extravagant quality

The following is a list of the most common times that particular items come on sale. If you can put off a needed purchase until the sale arrives you may find some good bargains.

Appliances - January, March, July, October
Autos - August, September, November, December
Bedding - January, August
Bicycles - January, September
Building materials - June
Carpets - February, July
Clothing - January, August
Fishing equipment - April, October
Furniture - January, July
Housewares - January, August
Stereos - January, May
TV's - May, June
White goods - January, May, August

Shopping to Eat

Would it be surprising to you if I told you that almost 25% of the money spent in the supermarket is for non-food items. Paper, soap, health, beauty aids, liquor, etc. account for close to 25% of the tab at the checkout stand. So when itemizing your preliminary budget you will find that supermarket money will be projected most accurately by adding an allowance of 30% to your pure food budget amount. You will notice that supermarkets are becoming more like the old general store. Everything from oil for your car to perfumes is being offered at the local supermarket. So beware of those aisles that do not have the items you want on your list.

The facts show that nearly a majority of Americans are getting a poor diet. The culprit seems to be sugar. People are increasing the amount received from starches. Too much sugar is not good for you. A high sugar breakfast for example will give you a quick burst of energy then let you down with the 11 o'clock droopies. A protein and starch cereal will also give you a quick burst of energy but will not let you down with that burned out feeling later.

Food Buying Guidelines

1. Plan - your meals and your shopping

2. List - use a list. It is convenient and saves time.

3. Shop - once a week on a full stomach. Shopping for food on an empty stomach only courts temptations for expensive gourmet items and snacks.

4. Buy - items that you may purchase at convenience stores can be purchased at substantial discounts in the supermarket.

5. Snacks - are expensive in general

6. Prices - National brands are more expensive than store brands usually.

7. Economy sizes are economical if all the contents are used without wasteful leftover or spoilage.

8. Seasons - create cheap prices in the summer for fruits and

various other times for vegetables. Satisfy yourself during the peak of the harvest when it's cheapest.

9. Meat - is expensive and too many of us indulge in huge steaks. Check the amount of fat and bone compared to the meat.

10. Compare - brands of the same item. Sometimes cheaper is better.

11. Clerks - watch them and count your change.

Restaurants

From fast food to chateau briand restaurants cost more than home prepared food. The reason is simple, you are paying for the service provided in the preparation and serving of a meal. The same meal at a restaurant can cost from 10 to 100% more than the same food prepared at home. Restaurants can be economical when what you are ordering is the kind of dish that would involve the purchase of numerous food items that you would not normally buy and that will have portions unused and wasted due to the specialized nature of the dish. Restaurants are also economical if time is money for you and the time wasted preparing a meal could be better spent earning money. In other words if you were in and out of a restaurant in 20 minutes and it would have taken you an hour to prepare and eat the meal yourself, the difference of 40 minutes at $15 per hour would mean that you could spend much more for your meal in a restaurant and the difference to you would be winding up with more money than if you had taken a full hour with self service (assuming that the 40 minutes is extra work).

33

Liquor is one of the biggest items in restaurants. If you can nurse your drink or avoid alcoholic drinks altogether while dining, you will realize a considerable saving. Wine is one of the real profit makers for restaurant owners. With the price usually double of what normal retail prices are, you may want to have your wine at home.

Organic Food

Organic food is probably better for you if you can afford it. The strict definition of organic food is that food that is grown without the use of pesticides and chemical fertilizers. The theory is that such foods will be pure food, free of any contaminants and therefore your health will be maintained at its highest. The problem is that food grown under such conditions has a much lower productivity factor, so it costs more. Another problem is that with the development of sincere and professional organic growers and distributors has come a plague of frauds by those who label foods as organic that do not meet the true criteria. Be sure you buy your organic food from a reputable organic market and read the labels for contents to be sure that what you buy is indeed pure. Just because a label says ''organic'' does not guarantee anything. Study the labels of the various foods you buy regularly until you know which ones are indeed organic or as close as you can get.

The excessive amounts of fat, sugar, salt, cholesterol and alcohol that make up the eating habits of too many people have been related to cancer of the stomach, breast, prostrate, liver and intestines. Another study indicates that those people contracting heart disease, angina, diabetes, and arthritis, were able to overcome the symptoms of these diseases in 90 days on a low fat, low sugar, high carbohydrate diet and a program of regular moderate exercise.

I take the time to go through the basics of a diet because properly prepared, a good diet will save you plenty in the way of shopping bills, by eliminating junk food and the potential savings in medical bills is astronomical!

Carbohydrates

Carbohydrates are grain products, vegetables, and sweets. The complex carbohydrates are grain and vegetables and are most important in your diet. Sugar use has been linked to diabetes and cholesterol. To the extent that grain and vegetables replace calories in your diet obtained from sugar and fats, they are most important. Contrary to popular belief that grain products will put weight on, is the fact that a lack of these products will contribute to a need to replace these essentials with harmful substitutes such as sugar and fat products.

Fat

Fat is an important part of the diet and is a necessary part of the diet. The problem in America with fats is the excessive use in the diet to the exclusion of complex carbohydrates. the excessive use of fat, especially animal fat in beef, veal and pork leads to high cholesterol and obesity, the most common causes of heart problems.

Protein

The highest source of protein are meat, fish, poultry, eggs, milk, and grains. The most efficient sources of protein are grains.

Vitamins

Vitamins can be broken down into two groups: fat soluble and water soluble. The fat soluble vitamins (A, D, E and K) are stored in the body and need not be replenished as often as the water soluble vitamins. Since the fat soluble vitamins are stored in the body it is possible to have an overdose. The water solubles (C, B-1, B-2, B-6, B-12 etc.) are found most often in vegetables; especially leafy vegetables and grains.

THE U.S. RECOMMENDED DAILY ALLOWANCES (RDA)

Protein—65 grams
Vitamin A—5000 units
Vitamin C—60 mg.
Vitamin B-1 Thiamin—1.5 mg.
Vitamin B-2 Riboflavin—1.7 mg.
Vitamin B-6 Pyridoxine—2.00
Vitamin B-12 Cobalamin—6 mcg
Vitamin D—400 units
Vitamin E—30 units

Freezers

Unless you live in a remote area or on a farm, the supposed savings of buying bulk and storing in a freezer will most often get eaten up in the cost of purchasing the freezer, the cost of operating the freezer (especially with electric bills climbing), and waste. Freezer plans that include the purchase of the side of beef are often aimed at the ignorant consumer with claims

that the "saving from bulk buying will pay for the freezer".
Often these plans are offered with lowdown financing and
high interest rates. Don't get caught in that game-rip-offs oc-
cur and if it was really such a deal everybody would have one.
Fraud and deceptive practices abound in the beef-freezer
business.

Liquor

Beer, Wine, and liquors can be a source of considerable
savings. Below is a list of the way to save:

Find a good "house brand". You can always pour from a
decanter.

Buy in bulk or large containers.

Limit drinking especially outside the house where you may
have to drive.

Buy on sale.

Measure your Drinks.

With mixed drinks you can usually get away without a name
brand.

Price liquor by the ounce.

Clothing

Buying clothes is like buying anything else today, in order
to get the best value for your dollar you must follow the fun-

damentals.

1. Follow your budget.

2 .Make the decision to buy at home-don't buy on impulse.

3. Shop carefully and thoroughly until you know the merchandise.

4. Make the purchase on the best terms for you.

Clothes buying is a specialized process though, and the following guidelines and methods will make your clothing budget work efficiently.

1. Allocate a certain amount to each person in the family rather than an overall figure. Women and girls typically spend more for clothes.

2. Plan your wardrobe. The best way to begin your plan is to take an inventory of what you presently have.

3. Buy your seasonal clothing well in advance. Winter clothing should be purchased in early fall and summer clothes in early spring.

4. Underclothes, socks, stockings etc. are best bought on sale.

5. A few high quality clothes are better and will be a better value than lots of cheap clothes in general. High quality does not necessarily mean the most expensive. Check the seams, buttons, button holes, type of material and zippers.

6. Buy a wardrobe that is color coordinated. Stick to the more standard type and avoid fad clothing.

7. Rapidly growing children should pass their clothes on to smaller children. Friends and relatives with children may be a good source of clothing.

8. Adults know your sizes. Write your size down and keep it with your records. Always try on clothes to make sure they fit properly. Different styles and brands do vary.

Clothes Care Costs

Proper maintenance of your wardrobe will keep your clothing its best for the longest time. Cutting costs of cleaning as well as preserving longevity can be effected by purchase of easy care clothing and quality clothing. Here are some tips for care of clothing.

1. Permanent press fibers are the easiest to care for. To get the most out of these fabrics, wash in small loads; immediately put them in the dryer at the low temperature setting and when they are dry immediately put them on a hanger. Buttoning the top two buttons will keep shirt collars from wrinkling. Pants should be hung up by their full length.

2. Most clothes that recommend dry cleaning can be hand washed.

3. Dry cleaning bills can be reduced by dry cleaning at coin operated dry cleaners.

When using stain removers always read the directions and

test the product in an inconspicuous place on the garment. Let it dry to be sure that the stain remover does not also remove the fabric!

Appliances

Appliances are another set of nifty items that require care before selection. Almost all appliances are labor saving devices except TV's and stereos. To be sure you are getting a labor saving device, check carefully the quality of the appliance. Check with others to find out their experiences with a potential purchase. The best place to check is the Consumer's Union rating service. This is a periodical with monthly issues and special annual reports on products. The service reports the brand name and model number for a wide range of appliances test results. With this service you can call a number of stores with the brand and model number you found best in your price range and request a price. So simply by checking at the local library in the Consumer's Union report and a number of phone calls you are fully prepared to enter an appliance store or department and make your judgements about the appliance based on a demonstration. If everything checks out you can buy confidently, knowing that you have done a good job of shopping.

Try to buy appliances on sale where discounts of 10-30% are significant dollar amounts $5 to $60 and more, can be saved. But beware of sales or discounts at stores that perpetually discount items. Again if you have checked around sufficiently, you will know if an item is a bargain. Model clearance sales usually are genuine sales. Floor models should be adequately discounted. Ask how long its been on the floor. Discounts should be at least 10% if you cannot see anything wrong and more if there is some damage. Used appliances can be a rip-off if you do not buy from a reputable dealer who will warrant the product. As-is deals are strictly luck if you get a good deal. Also used items should be substantially discounted from the new price. Paying more than ½ or ⅓ of the new price should be a maximum.

T.V.'s

I have provided some guidelines to be used in the purchase of a television.

1. Make your decision regarding whether or not you need a new TV and if it will fit the budget at this time.

2. Become familiar with the various models and features and their prices. Use a note pad to take notes for comparison.

3. Find out about the warranty.

4. Check the picture for clarity and distortion.

5. Determine what type of antenna you will need. Color TV sets require larger antennas.

6. Make sure the brand you buy has adequate service in your region or the region you may be moving to. If you don't have an authorized service center in your area, repairs will be costly and time consuming.

7. Here are some further considerations to cope with after you get to this point:

— Buy solid state circuitry.

— Check the specifications for the numbers of IF stages-it should have 3.

— Make sure the set will fit in with your decor at your home.

—Do not lease or rent a TV, the rates are usually equal the payments you would make if you had bought it new. If you need a TV temporarily you can usually find a used one that works in the paper or at the store for about $30. Unless you need your TV for less than 3 months it will probably be cheaper to buy a used set.

Stereo

Stereophonic equipment sales is a highly competitive field so you should be extra careful to shop around for a set that will suit your requirements. Stereo equipment is offered in AM and FM radios, record players, tape players, eight track, and cassette players, portable models and combinations of the above. In short, you name it in stereo and you can buy it.

To get an idea about what you want, first go to several stores and try out some of the equipment and compare some prices. When you have decided on what quality of sound you want—go to the library and check the Consumer's Union Reports. Then compare prices and look for sales till you feel ready to make the purchase.
Remember—

— Records are cheaper than tapes.

— The cassette is considered to be trouble free compared to the 8 track.

— The system will be as strong as its weakest component.

— Service can be very important.

—Turn the sound up to check distortion in the system and speakers.

Repairs

The first thing to do is check in your records for the warranty to see what the warranty covers. This, of course, assumes that your appliance really needs repair. To be sure it does need repair, go through this checklist to save time and money:

— Plug—is it plugged in?

— Check the fuses in machine (after you unplug it) and in the circuit

— Ask someone with a mechanical aptitude to look at it to see what can be done.

If the above fails to produce the desired results, contact a few reliable repair people and ask them what they think it is, what it will cost to fix, and what the part costs and what their hourly rates are. How far you get with these questions and what you are able to compare will tell you who to take the appliance to. Always bring the appliance in if possible, it's cheaper.

Get an estimate from the repair people before they start work. You are entitled to such an estimate. Or ask them to call you if repairs are more than $5 or $10. If the estimate is too high, you will definitely want to get another opinion because it may be cheaper in the long run to buy a new appliance.

Utilites And Energy

Your utility bills have undoubtedly increased in the last few years and the energy crunch only promises higher fuel electricity bills in the future. A geometric increase in worldwide energy use, and limited technology, indicate that the future holds shortages and increased prices for you in the years to come.

To hedge against such an eventuality and current bill, there are several things you can do to save. Incidently, if you own your own home, making such improvements as outlined here will increase the value of your home and make it more comfortable to live in.

1. Install storm windows to cut heat loss, through glass windows, one of the worst offenders in heat loss. Also buy heavy drapes and close them at night.

2. Insulate your attic. You can do this yourself or hire a contractor. Many utility companies have programs for financing and contracting the insulation of your attic. Saving may run as much as 25% per year. Be wary of private contractors and as in any contract get the correct specifications and put it all down in the contract estimate. Get several estimates and pick the one that gives you the most value for your money. Insulation varies in quality from R-22 that should be a minimum of 10" thick to R-11 which should be at least 5" thick. Make

your contractor prove that he is bonded and that his workers are covered for disability-if he is not covered, you may be liable for damages and/or injuries.

3. Use weatherstripping or caulking around doors and windows to prevent drafts and heat loss.

4. Let the sun shine on your house. If folliage, trees and awnings are blocking the sun from hitting your house, you will profit by trimming and removing these things that block the sun from warming your house.

5. If you have a swimming pool, get a cover for it to save 30% of heating cost. Turn the heater off in winter months and "spot" heat if you plan to use it one weekend. The optimum pool temperature is 78 degrees, according to the American Red Cross, but you can reduce your pool heating costs 25% by keeping the temperature at 75 degrees. Use an immersion bulb thermometer to measure in your pool. Better than all the above is to invest in a reliable solar heater for your pool. Do be thorough in your investigation of solar heaters as there are many that do not measure up to reasonable standards. Also, do not store pool chemicals in the same structure as your heater as these chemicals are highly corrosive and combustible.

The Phone Bill

People complain most often about the amount of their phone bill, yet by following a few simple rules your bill can be substantially reduced.

— Dial long distance yourself. Collect, person to person etc.

45

are sometimes double or more of regular rates.

— Take advantage of the lower rates advertised in the evenings and early morning hours.

— Organize what you are saying.

— Write a letter if this is practical.

— Get credit for reaching a wrong number on long distance calls. Just tell the operator.

— Use your home phone instead of expensive pay phones.

Safety

Exercising safety measures will prevent accidents that can be costly not only in terms of dollars and time, but most important to your health. Taking the time to go through the following lists may be one of the most important steps in your lifetime. Your health is the most important thing. So do it now while you are reading.

Fire Protection

Smoking, matches, wiring, appliances, heating equipment, and chimneys are the leading causes of fires in the United States today. Check your personal habits to see if you are playing with fire. As a means to cut back on smoking some of my friends have decided not to smoke in the bedroom.

— Is your house or apartment equipped with enough ashtrays or do you leave your cigarette sitting on the counter where it

46

can be inadvertently knocked on the floor to start a fire?

— Make sure appliances are working properly and that wires and plugs are not frayed, dried or cracked.

— Service your furnace or heating system once a year per service instructions and clean the filter monthly.

— Keep a fully charged fire extinguisher available and make sure everyone can use it.

— Check with the local fire department to determine the best extinguisher type for you. Do not use water type on electric fires; you could be shocked.

— Keep your chimney clear and get an approved fire screen.

— Do not put a heavier fuse in your electric box unless you check it out with a qualified electrician. Fuses are put there to stop overloads; Don't defeat this safety feature.

— Fuses or circuit breakers continually go out or appliances do not operate properly. Make an appointment to have an electrician check out your system for your safety and peace of mind.

— Use non-flammable cleaning agents.

— Remove old newspapers and oily rags that may begin burning on their own.

— GET a smoke detector that is approved by UL, and your local fire department.

Household Safeguards

Thousands die each year from accidents around the house including falls down the stairs, from the roof, off ladders, in the shower, through glass doors and on loose rugs. Use caution in these matters by providing adequate lighting on stairs. Put a non-slip pad in the shower. Check out glass doors for safety and if necessary put decals, available in variety stores, on the glass doors. Secure rugs to the floor.

Children are often the victims of other's neglect for safety. Haul off old refrigerators, take the door off or wire it shut. Keep cleaning liquids, medicines, garden chemicals, soaps and the like out of reach and locked up from children.

Pests can be a real problem in the house and garden if they are not taken care of. It is possible to control some insects without the heavy toxic pesticides.

Aphids—Lady bugs eat aphids as well as mites. Lacewings also eat aphids and mites and moth eggs. Preying Mantises will eat any insect smaller than itself.

Cockroaches—Sprinkle boric acid powder in the infected area or put the powder in crumbs in area.

Flys—Fly swatter, fly paper are effective. Make fly paper with molasses spread on paper.

Fleas—Try a flea collar made of eucalyptus seed.

Many carcinogens remain on the market despite tests proving their cancer-causing characteristics. Some are still on the market because the tests have been contradicted by other tests. And others are generally accepted as being carcinogenic in high doses, yet remain on the market. For instance, the government allows Red dye No. 4 in Maraschino cherries because they figure that the average person will not consume too many cherries, 4 a day!! To reduce your chance of cancer avoid or do the following:

— Drink purified water.

— Avoid excessive use of cosmetic and skin preparations that are suspected of being carcinogenic.

— Avoid use of poisonous and carcinogenic chemicals.

— Do not smoke any substance.

— Do not eat bacon or meats like hot dogs containing sodium nitrate.

— Clean vegetables thoroughly.

— Do not eat beef liver where DES accumulates. Women should not take DES.

— Do not sit closer than 6 feet from a color TV set and check with the US Consumer Product Safety Commission to see if your old set emits too much radiation.

— Avoid x-rays if possible and have a lead shield placed on you to protect your organs. Radiation has a cummulative effect. Make sure your microwave oven does not leak radiation.

— Wear an approved filter breathing mask when working in a dusty area or where the air is clogged with heavy particles.

Burglary

Burglaries have always been a serious problem so take preventive measures to increase your chances against being a victim of burglary!

Be especialy careful during the holiday when burglaries increase. Use a dead bolt on all wood doors and get a "pin" to lock sliding glass doors.

If you go on vacation use a timed light to turn on lights and a radio in the evening, have a neighbor pick up the mail and papers, and notify the police your departure and expected time of return.

Have a peephole put in your door to see who is there. Participate in Operation Identification and put a sticker in your window.

Consider a burglar alarm system and dobermans (dogs), if you keep valuable artwork and jewelry at home.

Check the reputation of those working around your home (remember casual labor should be insured.)

Sending Packages

Freight rates vary considerably depending on the carrier, speed of delivery you desire, and convenience. Be sure your package is well wrapped preferably in cardboard with heavy paper and twine. Write the address with a felt pen and put a return address and point of origin on the package. Insure fragile or valuable contents.

Check with the various services available to see what the particulars are for what you are sending and where you are sending it.

Bus

Bus service involves taking your package to the bus station and having the recipient pick it up. The most efficient bus service is between large cities at a short distance. If you are sending across long distances, the bus services will take more time as the package will have to be transfered.

Parcel Delivery Services

The large carriers provide door to door delivery and have numerous services beside the standard delivery. All are relatively efficient and fast. If the recipient is not at the address when the service attempts a delivery, then a note will be left and several more attempts made. Finally if the service cannot deliver to the recipient or a neighbor, the recipient may have to pick it up.

U.S. Postal Service

Parcel post is the cheapest and therefore slowest service offered by the Post Office. However, if you have planned ahead far enough, this economical service will provide entirely adequate service.

Priority mail is processed by hand as compared to machine with parcel post and is therefore faster and more expensive.

Express mail service will guarantee delivery in about a day and one-half or give a full refund. This is the US Post Office's fastest service and is expensive. However, the difference between 50 miles and 2,000 miles is only a couple of dollars.

To Your Health

High medical prices have been the subject of much discussion and complaining, yet, you the consumer are one of the primary causes. You demand excellent care and if something goes wrong are quick to serve a "Notice you have been sued!" paper on your physician. Generally physicians are very well trained and ethical people-most suits don't pay off. However, this barrage of suits has increased your health bill with higher malpractice insurance premiums and extensive double checking on diagnoses. High quality care means increased accuracy in diagnoses and shorter stays in the hospital with a better chance of living a normal life in the event of a serious illness. If hospitals are now $100/day and you stay two days, that's better than $50/day and a four day stay.

The average person visits the doctor about 5 times a year for various reasons and the dentist once or twice a year. You should budget yourself and family members for this amount and have a sufficient amount in your emergency fund to cover medical emergencies that are not covered under your insurance plan.

There are ways to reduce the amount spent on medical services if not the services. Find a doctor who is competent and reputable. If you are new in town and cannot get recommendations from satisfied patients whom you know, then check with the local medical society for a doctor who is listed on the staff of a good hospital or clinic (not necessarily large). Having your own doctor is most important in saving money as only your doctor knows your history. Often minor complaints can be handled over the phone without having to make a visit.

Do not ask for house visits unless absolutely necessary. Let the doctor determine this. House calls are expensive. Physicians fees should be discussed so that you know what the charge will be, and if you know what the charge will be, and if you have some difficulty in paying, arrangements can sometimes be made for a reduction in fee or terms cut check this out first. It will put you in a better position.

Get an annual physical exam especially if your family or you have had a history of serious illnesses. The essentials of a physical will include:

Blood Pressure, Breast examination, Pap smear, Eye Examination, Urinalysis, Stool analysis and Blood test.

Shop for a hospital to find one that provides the most services for the least charge. Unfortunately doctors do not associate with all hospitals and limit their associations. Check with your doctor to see which hospitals he is associated with so you can compare services. A university teaching hospital will generally have a more sophisticated staff. If you have to use an emergency room or an ambulance your choice will depend on the amount of service provided and the rates. Some are going to provide the same services for less.

Surgery is a major expense and though most of us are covered by insurance, it is not the sort of thing you just say OK to. Major abuses have occured in the recommendation of surgeries as indicated by differences in rates of surgery for different states—some have over 1000% differences in the rates of surgery. If surgery is recommended to you, get an independent opinion. Find a specialist on your own and tell him you want an opinion only, that he definitely will not be performing the surgery if it is indicated.

Many people are having cosmetic surgery in this modern age. If you are vain enough to proceed with such an operation be sure that you get a thoroughly reputable physician who specializes in the particular surgery of your desire. Check with your regular physician for a recommendation and be sure to see if the doctor is board certified and call the County Clerk to see if he is named in any malpractice suits.

Drugs

You can save considerably on prescription drugs by 1. shopping for a pharmacy and 2. asking your doctor to use generic names for prescriptions. Generic named drugs are up to 500% cheaper than brand named drugs. The chemical composition is the same only the name has been changed because the drug is marketed by a different company. Pregnant women should be very cautious about taking drugs of any kind. Evidence has linked the use of drugs, alcohol, nicotine and aspirin to abnormal babies. Give the kid a chance to decide for himself what drugs he wants. Drugs are most dangerous in the first three months of pregnancy.

Most over the counter drugs are used to aid healing or ease pain. Always read the precautions on the label. Simply put: some work and some don't. Aspirin is the most effective for many ailments. Antacids will do the job. Acne preparations main job is to cleanse the skin and this can be done effectively with an antibacterial soap. First aid ointments containing Bacitracira, Polymixin B sulfate with a complementary drug and tetracycline are effective. Antiperspirant manuafacturers were sweating in 1973 when problems with sirconium surfaced. The common cold has no cure and mustard oil, oil of turpentine, expectorant ingredients, anticholinergics ingredients are considered not safe and effective. Diet aids are considered not safe and effective. Hearing aids should be recommended by a doctor. Most sleeping pills are not very effective and should not be taken often.

Birth Control

If you do not practice the most effective form of birth control (no intercourse) and yet do feel responsible for any life that may be forth coming there are several methods to exercise control.

Oral contraceptives are the most effective means of control and they are relatively inexpensive but there are drawbacks such as increases in the chances of serious illness such as stroke and heart problems.

After oral contraceptives and ranking very close, IUD's (intrauterine devices) are the next most effective means of contraception and after that in order are prophylactic devices, diaphragms with cream or jelly alone. The risk of death from childbirth is less in all contraceptives above except with oral contraceptives for women over 40 years old.

Vasectomy, hysterectomy, and other contraceptive operations are also an alternative and in the case of a vasectomy may be cheaper in the long run. Operations are generally permanent.

Buying a Car

The purchase of an automobile represents a substantial investment for most families and should therefore be the object of intense scrutiny. Knowing what you can afford, shopping the market place, and negotiating the sale are the basic components of a successful purchase. Since buying a car is a large purchase large savings can be had or large losses can be the result of being had.

Decide whether you want a new car or a used car first. New cars represent the best automobile: trouble free driving and the most modern comfort and safety—new cars also cost the most. The variety of used cars is endless. For the same price as a new compact you can get an older large car. Used cars are cheaper than new cars but a used car is a used car, i.e. it has been driven X miles, has X dents, and has X miles left to drive. The easiest way to decide if you want a new or a used car is to decide the type of car large-small, sport-sedan etc. When you put type and price together it will be evident whether a new or used is the way to go. If you need help deciding what you can afford in the way of monthly payments call or drop by your bank and tell your loan officer what you are considering in the way of dollars in payments then ask what you can qualify for. The bank loan officer will need to know if you are considering a new or used car so be prepared. Often the bank will make a tentative commitment for a loan of x dollars or x percentage of value at specified rate usually 11 to 15% APA at x $$ per month for x months. (See chart page 58)

Go to the library and look up the Consumer's Union reports. Also check the other auto magazines for their reports on new cars.

Now you are ready to seriously look at and test drive the makes you have decided on for a closer inspection. Take your paper with you and fill out your information for each make. You will have to get the salesman's help with the final price-out the door. Don't be afraid to show him your sheet. If anything the sheet will indicate that you are a serious buyer who is knowledgeable so you will get better service. If you don't get good sales help and the salesman tries to discount your comparison approach, there is a good probability that he knows his make will not compare favorably. This may not always be the case but it is something to look out for, because an experienced salesman will know if his car is the deal in a particular class. However, do not be so naive as to believe it if he tells you he has the best deal. Just get a complete written price: tax, license, preparation, extras, as you want, and take a test drive. Thank the man as you note the results.

Getting a bargain price on a new car can be an exhilarating experience. The bargain price you might have guessed, is somewhat lower than the sticker or suggested retail price. Dealers mark up small cars about 15%, intermediate and

A New Car

Once you have decided on a new car the next big question becomes what size, make, engine, doors, radio etc. you want. Decide a size class first: luxury to sports, compacts etc. Price will help to determine this for you.

Make a list of the features you want on a large sheet of paper.

	Make 1		Make 2		Make 3		Make 4	
	dealer 1	dealer 2	dealer 1	dealer 2	dealer 1	dealer 2	dealer 1	dealer 2
Price total								
Miles per gallon								
Foreign/domestic								
Service Available								
Consumer's Union								
Warranty								
Test Drive								

standard about 20% and luxury about 25%. Accessories are marked up about 50%. To figure what you should pay, add up:

— Base price (Intermediate)	4200
20% Mark up	− 840
	3360
Accessories total	+ 700
— 50% of 700	4060
	− 350
Dealer's Approx cost	3710
Dealer's Profit (5-15%)	+ 370
	4080
Dealer Preparation & Freight	+ 200
Price you want to pay	4280
(Plus tax & License) Sticker Price	(5100)

You won't always get such a discount but if you shop during the slack months during a blizzard, during an advertised special you should be able to get a good price.

Trade Ins

If you have the time and are willing to sell your own car, it is possible to make money by selling your car yourself rather than trading it in. But make these considerations first:

— What can you sell the car for?

— What will advertising cost? Try free papers and word of mouth.

— How much time will it take?

— What will a dealer give me for it? (In some states trade ins reduce the price of the car and the amount of sales tax paid. Hence, if you were to get $2000 plus 6% or $2,120 selling it yourself plus advertising and your time.)

— Maybe you can get more selling it yourself.

Used Cars

When purchasing a used automobile one of the most important questions to answer is who am I dealing with? You can buy a used car either from a dealer or a private party. With either one you will have to be cautious and keep a wary eye for fast talk. Check with the Better Business Bureau for complaints about your prospective dealer. Usually the used car lots that are part of a major dealership will be the most reputable and have the best cars.

Since most of the depreciation in a car happens in the first year or two it makes sense that a two year old, well maintained automobile may be a good place to start looking at used cars.

Know the value of your prospective car. Your bank will show you the range of values in a book of used car price averages. Look at several, at least 4, of the type of car which you want to compare prices and conditions.

	#1	#2	#3	#4
Where Seen				
Year and Model				
Miles				
Price				
Tires				
Battery				
Brakes				
Interior				
Paint/Body				
Clutch/Transmission				
Testdrive/engine				

Invest in a mechanic's opinion before closing the deal. A mechanic can not only tell you how your prospective car is running but how much the car is worth to some degree. Always read your purchase agreement thoroughly. Warranties are something you ask for after you get a written price because a dealer will otherwise boost the price to meet the cost of a warranty.

Leasing An Auto

There are two ways to lease an automobile basically, closed end and open end leases. The closed end lease is generally more expensive as the lessee makes a fixed monthly payment for the term of the lease, where in the less expensive open end lease the lessee carries some of the risk. The risk is carried by the lessee because under an open end lease the lessee agrees to a residual value for the car at the end of the lease. If the car cannot be sold for the residual value, then the lessee will have to pay the difference. On the other hand if the car is worth more than the residual value, the lessee will receive the difference.

To compare leases check these features in the agreement:

Maintenance
Insurance
Tire Replacement
Dents
Excess mileage
Lease cancellation
Initial costs
Monthly payment
Residual value (open end only)

Leasing can be cheaper if you buy a new car every year or two and/or you use your car strictly for business. If you keep your car for three years or more it will generally be cheaper to buy. The advantages to leasing are no downpayment, and very little bargaining.

Vacation Time

Take your time shopping for a vacation. It will not only save you money; it will be an enjoyable experience. Half the fun of taking a vacation is getting there and half the savings can be generated by knowing how to get the bargains in transportation. The other half of savings can be had in the form of savings on meals and lodging. The easiest and most convenient way to find out what is available is to find a good travel agent.

Travel Agents

The best way to determine if you are working with a reliable agent is to check on the prices he quotes you. The best way to find a competent agent who is knowledgeable about all the tours is to compare responses of several agents to the same questions regarding a particular vacation you have planned.

If you decide a travel agent is not for you and you want to make all your own arrangements, you will find that it may be easier for weekend holidays to nearby locations you are familiar with. Far away locations particulary overseas destinations will require quite a bit of investigation and the agent can help you out considerably in this respect.

Air

The largest savings can be effected by booking well in advance in economy class. First class can be ⅓ to ½ more expensive. Flying at night, during the week, and during off season can also save you money. There are a multitude of bargain air fares-your travel agent can point you in the right direction.

Rail

Amtrack, this nation's passenger rail service, has modernized and upgraded train service throughout the country. Fares are competitive with air transportation. Check your local directory for the Toll free number.

If you plan to use a Eurailpass for traveling in Europe be sure to get it in the United States-it will be too late if you want to get that bargain transportation in Europe because its only available in the U.S. So buy before you go so that you will have it when you get there.

Hotels

Parks are the cheapest "hotels" but if you want more comfort or are staying in a large city, having a convenient, clean, and perhaps plush accomodations will make your stay nicer. To assure proper accomodations always 1) be familiar with the hotel and the area it's in and 2) make reservations and give yourself plenty of time to check in. The newest and most modern hotels will be the most expensive. If you're just driving through why not pick out the least expensive accomodations that will suit your taste.

NOTES

65

Chapter Three

THE NOT SO HUMBLE ABODE

Whether you are a renter or a home owner, you will find significant savings in this chapter. Making the correct rent or buy decision, locating in the right area, and getting a good deal on your residence will make your life a lot easier in terms of time and money. Read this chapter so you'll be aware of what is available to you. The one thing that comes up most often in deciding where and what you want to live in is emotion. Do try to be kind to yourself by making your decisions on a rational basis. Becoming overly emotional will only confuse you and make a rational decision that much harder.

The Rent or Buy Decision

You must ask yourself several questions to make this decision. All of these questions will help to answer the big question: Should I buy now? It is a matter of simple arithmetic that owning is cheaper than renting in the long run.

How long will you be at your new location? If you are going to be 2½ years or more in that location generally it is safe to assume that buying will be cheaper. If you have a job with frequent transfers you may want to rent rather than have to sell your house in a hurry. You may also want your company to pay you for the loss of not owning your own home.

Can you afford to own your own home? The best way to find an answer to this question is to call your local mortgage company or bank. The second part of the answer to this question is another question: How steady is your income? If you are in an industry with frequent long layoffs you should have an adequate emergency fund in your budget to cover housing expense during such a time. There is nothing worse than having to move because of financial circumstances.

Do you want and are you ready to take on the responsibility of payments on a loan for a house? If you are well situated in your job, life style, etc. you may well be ready to buy. If you are not and you feel like your circumstances might change, then you might reconsider.

Financing

Since most of us do not pay cash for the entire price of our homes we must finance at least some of it. The loan that is used to borrow money to purchase your home is generally called a mortgage. Technically the mortgage is a security instrument (document) that protects the lender in the event of a default (non-payment on the loan). There are many types of loans available and shopping for the best deal can really be a money saver.

Conventional Loans

A Conventional loan is a loan made through a savings institution without any special government program. This type of loan requires from 5% to 30% of the purchase price as a down payment with 20% being an average down payment. Since there is no special government program guaranteeing these loans to the lender, the borrower will not be able to borrow as much given a certain income as he would under FHA or VA program. The greatest advantage of conventional loans is that you can get them on almost any property, they don't cost the seller anything, and they can be processed quicker, typically 30 vs 60 days for FHA or VA guaranteed loans.

FHA Loans

Under the Federal Housing Administration guarantee program, loans are guaranteed to the lender for the borrower. To get one of these loans just apply to a lender specifying that you want a FHA loan. FHA loans take about 60 days to process, cost the seller "points" (See Points) and the house must be appraised at the value you are paying or you may put down additional cash to make up the difference. Currently FHA requires as a down payment:

$$3\% \text{ of first } 25,000 = 750$$
$$5\% \text{ of next } 35,000 = 1750$$

Maximum 60,000 $2500 Downpayment plus
                                                           closing costs

VA Loans

The Veterans Administration guarantees loans to military personnel and veterans. These loans have about the same requirement and time schedule as the FHA program except that the program is limited to service people. The best thing about VA loans is **no** down payment, the only thing necessary for purchase is a good income and closing costs.

Assuming a Loan

The only loans you can assume are VA and FHA guaranteed loans. The person who lets his VA loan be assumed cannot get another VA loan and as with FHA remains primarily responsible for the loan in the event of a default. The big advantage of assuming a loan is that you do not have to qualify for the loan (i.e. have a certain income).

2nd Loans

A second mortgage may be taken at purchase of a property by a purchaser from the seller or anyone else if he has the permission of the lending institution making the main loan. VA and FHA programs do not allow 2nd mortgages at purchase. A 2nd mortgage may be taken after the property has appreciated enough for a lender to loan without risk.

Points

A point is one percent of the amount of a loan. Points are charged by lenders to buyers on conventional loans and to buyers and sellers on FHA loans. FHA and VA allow the buyer to pay only one point. The seller then has to pay from 1 to 10 points. Check with at least five lenders to determine what the going rate is.

Prepayment and Escrow

Be sure your loan has a prepayment privilege and if possible one without penalty. Sometimes up to six months interest is charged.

An Escrow company is charged with handling the money, deeds, title insurance, and loan payoffs. The escrow company is a neutral party instructed by you and the other party to the transaction, in escrow instructions to perform certain acts that are most safely and conveniently done by a professional neutral party.

Types of Houses

You can buy a new house, a used house, a condominium, cooperative apartment, mobile home, or you can build your own home, live in a retirement village, nursing home, apartment rental or rental house, and you might even try a houseboat. Whatever your choice is, you will have to make a go of it for some time probably, so before choosing consider a few of the pluses and minuses.

A Used Home

A used home is ready to move into and live as compared to a new home where landscaping, carpets and drapes will need to be taken care of. Used homes generally provide a superior location in terms of being close to work and shopping and the city. Most used homes are mechanically fine. A simple check of plumbing, heating, and appliances by operating each yourself before buying will reassure you of their operability. If something does not work or looks like it wil break down any minute, consider the price you are paying. It may be wise to ask for a credit from the seller to replace the worn item(s). Your Realtor will be able to help you with this.

A New Home

Most new homes are located in the suburbs away from work and the hustle and bustle of a busy city. If you prefer the quiet and can afford the higher prices of a suburban (including extra the cost of commuting), a new house might be the ticket for you. Be aware that a custom house built on a single lot will be more expensive than a comparable tract home. Developers save money by building in quantity and pass the savings along to you. Most used homes were once part of a tract but the differences in landscaping and care have made each one distinguished by the tastes of the family who landscaped it. Check the quality of construction, fixtures, and appliances in a new home for durability. Ask your lender about an allowance for basic improvements.

A Cooperative Apartment

A cooperative apartment is a group of people, who together in a corporation own and operate an apartment building. Each owner has a number of shares proportionate to the size of the apartment lived in. Each owner gets a lease on his apartment. Monthly expenses include the mortgage, taxes, and a monthly maintenance fee. The maintenance fee goes to a professional maintenance contract. Good maintenance will improve the value of your apartment.

A Condominium

A condominium is very similar to a cooperative apartment except that the technicalities of ownership are different. It is not a corporation, it is a group of individual owners. Condos are generally easier to buy because financing is easier to get. Be sure that the maintenance fee is adequate to take care of monthly charges and deferred expenses such as painting, roofs, driveways, care of and replacement of recreational facilities, etc.

71

A Mobile Home

A mobile home is the least expensive home you can purchase compared dollar for dollar with other types of homes. Mobile homes are set up in parks where you pay rent for the space you occupy. Be sure to check and compare the differences in parks. Some are set up for adults and some for families. Try to get the longest lease you can get to avoid a major pitfall of mobile home parks rent increases. If you have a fixed income or you are retired this can be a deciding factor. FHA and VA will guarantee loans on mobile homes. One easy rule of thumb to compare quality in comparable size homes is weight. Generally a heavier construction implies better quality. Also check the "Official Mobile Market Report" available from dealers for the value of your model of mobile home.

Building a Custom Home

You may want your very own custom home designed especially for you and your family. It is a major undertaking and should not be attempted unless you have lots of time and/or you know the most trusted and respected contractor in your area. Consider where you will build—in a subdivision of lots, in an existing neighborhood, or on acreage. How the area will develop in the future is of prime importance. Don't over build for a neighborhood. Check with you Realtor and architect on costs of development for a particular site, each will vary considerably.

Nursing Homes

A nursing home is a place for those who are recovering

from an illness or who are not able to take care of themselves for one reason or another. The costs and especially the quality of care vary considerably. If you are planning to enter a Nursing home or know someone that is, make a thorough investigation of the homes in your area. Talk to friends, relatives, and people in the medical profession for references as to getting the kind of care you need.

The Realtor and Others in Real Estate

A Realtor is a real estate broker with years of experience who is a member of a Realtor's association. Many people refer to anyone with a license to sell real estate as a "realtor". Knowing the difference between Realtor, Realtor Associate, broker and salesman will help you to choose someone who is most competent to perform the services of a real estate agent.

Realtor — the most competent designation of the Realtors Association.

Realtor Associate — one who works for a Realtor.

Broker — to become a broker one must have passed the salesman's license test, worked two years full time or taken a series of college level courses (requirements vary by state), and passed the brokers's license exam.

Salesman — anyone who has taken a cram course and passed the state examination.

Be sure to ask your potential estate agent exactly what his qualifications are. Real Estate is big money so you should try to be as knowledgeable as possible about the business and who you are dealing with. A quick call to the local board will help. The real estate agent's job is to coordinate the sale of your house; a formidable task for the uninitiated.

Lawyer

If you are working with a Realtor on a simple, uncomplicated sale of your house, a lawyer will probably be just an extra expense. If there is anything you do not understand in the contract or the sale has extra conditions or complications, tell your Realtor you would like to have your attorney look over the contract before agreeing to anything.

Loan Officer

The loan officer is the one who can best explain to you the means to finance the purchase of a home.

Insurance Broker

The insurance broker will recommend to you the type of insurance that you will need as a homeowner. A broker who handles more than one company will most likely be able to provide you with the best policy for your particular needs.

Escrow Officer

The escrow officer handles all the loan documents, insurance, taxes, recording fees, loan payoffs, transfer tax, etc. The escrow officer must do what you tell him to do in the escrow instructions.

Selling Your House

The job of selling your house is not an easy one and should be taken with great care. Selling your house yourself is not recommended. Using a professional real estate agent who has all the expertise to make the sale is an experience you won't later regret.

The most common and best method of selling is with an exclusive right to sell listing, using the multiple listing service. This agreement between you and your agent is the best incentive you can give your agent to go to work for you. Information regarding your house and terms of financing are published and distributed to members of the multiple listing service of the Realtor's board. You will want to specify that agents call to make an appointment or if you are away that a lock box device is used. A lock box is a special heavy duty metal box with copies of your keys inside placed on your property. Only members of the service can use the box because the box contains a lock opened only by special keys.

Make sure that a proper value has been assigned to your house by getting several opinions from Realtors and if necessary hire an independent appraiser to confirm the price. Always add about 5% to the appraised value so that you have room to bargain on the price. Adding too much will result in no offers being made. If you are really in a hurry to sell just add 1% or 2% over the appraised value estimate.

When potential buyers come to see your house make sure everything is in tip top shape. This will impress the buyers that you have maintained your house well. Minor fixing up such as gardening, paint trim (if needed) waxed floors, etc.

will go a long way towards closing a sale. Don't invest in a new roof or carpet, unless it really needs it.

Make the financing attractive to buyers by offering your house with conventional, VH, FHA, and 2nd mortgage financing. Some buyers may be looking exclusively for VA terms where they will have a zero downpayment. By offering all terms to your buyers your broker will be able to get a little better price perhaps and will certainly have a large market for prospects.

Shopping for a House

The first order of business is determining what type of house you want to live in - new, used, old, condo, mobile home, etc. Some of this will be determined by what size family you have, your income, and your personal preferences. After you have decided what kind of home you want you will want to find a location.

Where you live is just as important as what you want to live in. You should pick an area that suits your needs. Important needs and wants to consider are:

Income level of the neighborhood

Age—life cycle of residents

Proximity to work, schools, shopping, recreation

Quality of schools

Traffic patterns near your block

Exposure to the sun

Taxes

Character of neighborhood (new, old, changing)

Zoning

Freeway access

Availability of transportation lines

Drive several neighborhoods you are considering at various times to check these qualities. When you are satisfied with a neighborhood and you have chosen it to be the one you want you want to choose a Realtor who works in that area to help you find your home.

The Realtor will show you several homes and describe features and prices. Be sure to ask the Realtor to show and describe to you homes that have just recently sold so that you can get a good idea of value. By comparing prices you will get a reasonable idea. When looking through the homes the Realtor shows you take two large paper pads and pencils (one for each of you) and take notes:

	#1	#2	#3	etc.
Price	$60,000			
Address	419 Oak Drive			
Bedrooms	3 large master			
Baths	2 no counters			
Living Room	large, nice			
Dining Room	will fit table			

Kitchen	new floor
Features	all built ins/electric range
Family Room	No
Front Yard	lawn
Back Yard	OK easy care, rock & shrubs need trim
Patio/Balcony	covered patio
Paint interior	OK
exterior	OK
Carpets	OK
Laundry	220 V
Sewer	OK, City
Driveway	Cement
Garage	2 car, large
View	West over valley
Comments	Pretty good except landscaping

When you are ready to make an offer your realtor will assist you. He will need to know the type of loan you want, cash down, any special agreements, when you want possession, and personal property you believe should be included such as stove, carpets, drapes, dining room chandeliers, etc. Most states provide that the buyer name the title insurance company and the escrow company. Be sure you have personally shopped for these services as prices will vary. When making an offer, make it a fair price. "Low ball" offers are often not considered seriously by the seller.

Movers

The cheapest way to move your furnishings is by yourself or if you have been transfered by your company for your company to pay the costs. Such costs include the cost of selling, movers, cost of buying including an adjustment for location and mortgage rates.

If you have to pay the cost of moving yourself then you will want to get the best price. To shop for a moving company call a reputable company and ask for an estimate. An estimate cannot really be done over the phone in most cases. Insure your valuables and contents. Get an inventory list while packing and check it when you accept delivery. Don't let the movers wait at the new address or you will be charged extra. Also be prepared to pay in cash as checks generally are not accepted.

Maintaining and Improving Your Home

Once you finally have your own home you will find that there are numerous duties associated with the proper maintenance of your home. Knowing the basics of these chores will help you save money. If you decide that you want to improve your home with major work you will want to know that quality and prices vary considerably and that it does pay to shop for the best deal.

Landscaping

If you have bought a new home and are now faced with a yard that lacks a reasonable garden you will be faced with a question: do you want to spend a lot of time and/or money caring for your yard or do you want an easy care yard.

Easy care	Needs care
sprinklers	no sprinkler system
gravel or cement	no gravel or cement
trees and shrubs	lawn

ground cover   flower beds
fence   hedge

A yard can be designed to look nice with either set of options if done properly. Check the library for gardening books to give you a concept for design. You can use a professional landscape architect to get the best design and plant it yourself to save money.

Carpet

Buy your carpet from a reputable dealer during a sale and save a great deal. Beware of high pressure tactics as these firms may not be established or reputable. To judge quality in a carpet check:

Fiber: Wool —   the best and most expensive.

Acrylic —   very close in appearance and comfort. Be sure it has a good fire rating as all new carpet must.

Nylon —   more economical

Rayon —   wears poorly

Construction: Check the thickness, closeness of tufts, and strength of anchoring of tufts. This can be accomplished by pulling the tufts or looking at construction diagrams.

Color: Neutral or pastel is best. White is very hard to keep clean.

Drapes

Buy the strongest, quality drapery rods you can find to hang your drapes. Drapes should be twice as long as the rod they are hung from in order to assure fullness for most drapes. Be sure the color is coordinated to your furniture and carpet. Check this with an interior design coordinator or a salesperson at a reputable store (bring samples if possible).

Furniture

Furniture is a major expenditure - so much so that most people do not buy a houseful of furniture all at once. To get a set of furniture that suits your needs you will need a plan to fit into your budget and other plans. Consider these things: Young children can be hard on very nice furniture.

Buying furniture can be extra expensive if you plan to move soon, as the extra cost of moving the furniture must be added in. Even if it isn't a long distance move, your decor group may not fit well with the existing decor where you move.

Your used furniture can be used to decorate other rooms—for instance living room furniture bought now may be future family room furniture.

Used furniture can be a good buy. Check the papers and ask friends about possible sales.

Quality furniture is much better than cheap furniture.

Extravagantly designed or modern furniture designs may

go out of style.

Professional advice is available free from experienced, reputable sales people when they are not too busy. Visit these people at several stores during slack hours to discuss your needs and what will work best.

Contracting for Home Improvements

Be sure your home improvement is a worthwhile project—many people over build on their lots and find it hard to get their money out when they sell. Chances are if you need a variance from local zoning you should reconsider.

Adding a room, remodeling a kitchen or bathroom or just reroofing your house will take time and some skill. Look in magazines to find what you want and think about how it will fit in with what you have. Continuity is an important concept in home improvement.

Hiring the artisans is a job in itself. Doing it well will pay you in future enjoyment.

Architects — Ask what the fee is, what he specializes in, and the addresses of 4 or 5 completed jobs.

Contractors — Get the license number and check with the Better Business Bureau and state. Ask were he buys his supplies (for credit references). After all is checked get a detailed estimate and before work is started get a workman's compensation insurance voucher.

Casual labor —   Do not hire casual labor for skilled work. Be sure you have workman's compensation insurance coverage for casual labor. Call your agent to verify the coverage needed.

Many major improvements are financed by loans. Be sure you shop to get the best terms. Banks offer a number of programs. The government has special improvement loans. Bank lending officers can help you with what is currently available. If you finance through the contractor be aware that he will most likely sell the loan contract and that therefore you will be liable to the holder. Make sure your contract has payment possible upon completion of a satisfactory job per definition in the contract. Do not pay until the job is done right.

NOTES

Chapter Four

THE BANKS AND YOUR CREDIT

Having a bank that you like will bring you many pleasures throughout your lifetime. Getting the highest interest rate available, the best checking account, and convenient service will give you peace of mind and provide a framework for managing your money.

Shopping For a Bank

The following is a list of services available at the various savings institutions:

Checking accounts
Savings deposits
Time deposits (higher interest)
Payroll savings plan
Special savings plans (Christmas club, etc.)
Safe deposit boxes
Travelers checks
Money orders
Discount buying
Life insurance
U.S. savings bonds
Financial services (estate and trust management)
Home and home improvement loans
Auto, major appliance, vacation, etc. loans
Student, personal, business loans
Credit cards
Check guarantee cards
Bill payment

In addition to the above, you may want a bank that is close by, has drive-up windows, longer hours, or an automatic teller.

It is not necessary to have all your services at one bank, you may want the checking plan at one bank while still being able to save at another bank that pays higher interest. The best way to get the most for your money-and banks do charge money for their services—is to make a list of the services you need or want and then find the bank or banks that give you the best deal. The following will provide some basis for comparison and generally tells you what to look for in the way of bargain banking services and how to use the services provided.

Using Savings Accounts

The federal government sets the maximum interest rates that savings institutions can pay the various savings account types. Below are the maximum nominal interest rates permitted under federal regulation:

Account	Savings & Loans	Banks
Passbook	5.25%	5.00%
90 days	5.75%	5.50%
1 to 2½ years	6.50%	6.00%
2½ to 4 years	6.75%	6.50%
4 to 6 years	7.50%	7.25%
6 years or more	7.75%	7.50%

If you put your money in a time account beware of interest penalties for early withdrawal. The penalties are regulated by federal regulation also. For example if you deposit $10,000 into a 6 year time account earning 7¾% interest and you later decided to withdraw some of the money you would face a penalty. The penalty applies only to those funds that are withdrawn, it does not apply to interest left in the account only cash drawn against the original $10,000. If you withdrew $1,000, leaving $9,000, after two years, then you would be penalized 90 days interest on that $1,000 plus you would also get only a maximum of 5¼% interest over the two years. The other $9,000 would still be earning 7¾%.

Another thing to be careful of with time deposits is the difference between the stated interest rate and the "yield". The yield is the percentage accumulated over the time period if you leave the interest in the account. If you are comparing accounts for the amount of interest paid always ask for the annual percentage rate. The yield figure can be deceptive.

If you periodically withdraw money from a passbook savings account be sure that your bank is not charging you a service charge for withdrawal. Some banks have free withdrawal service. Also when you make your withdrawal, you should check with the bank to see if you are being paid interest up to the day of withdrawal as well as from the day of deposit. You should of course, take into account the other conveniences a savings institution offers as well as their fees and interest rates.

Insured Savings Accounts

If for any reason you are worried as to the amount of money that you can be insured for in a savings account and you are holding back earning it because you are afraid that there is no safe place to keep all that money, rest assured because the savings institutions can hold plenty, fully insured. For instance a man, a wife, and their children can safely deposit up to $1,400,000 in one insured savings institution. Of course, you would have to set up a number of different accounts. In addition this family could place this amount in accounts at different banks not branches of the same bank and receive the same amount of insurance coverage. The largest sum that can be placed in one account at one bank and still be insured is $100,000. Be sure that your banks are government insured—All that are insured advertise it.

Checking Accounts

It definitely pays to find a checking account that suits your needs. If you travel frequently you may want a bank that has branches that will cash checks in the area that you travel. Without such service it may become necessary to buy special travelers checks, carry large amounts of cash, and/or charge everything on a credit card.

When you are looking for a checking account be aware of the various plans so that you can ask for the kind of service you want.

Minimum Balance Account

Minimum Balance can be cheap or expensive. The way to figure how much it costs is to multiply the required minimum balance by the passbook interest rate. Thus a $300 minimum balance kept in a checking account could be earning $15.75 a year in a 5¼% savings account. This is your cost. If it costs $2 a month under another comparable plan then the difference is $8.25.

Per Check Account

With this account you are charged by the check and some charge a nominal minimum monthly service charge if you don't write enough checks. It's like a minimum charge at a restaurant table—you pay the minimum whether you order it or not. The charge helps to cover the cost of statements and bookkeeping.

Total Account

In this account you can get any number of services along with checking for a stated fee of between $2 and $3 a month. All the extra service may be nice IF you can use it.

NOW Account (Negotiable Order of Withdrawal)

NOW accounts are available in some states and they do pay interest on your account. Be sure to check into the real (Annual Percentage Rate) rate of interest paid.

Free Checking Account

Make sure there is no minimum balance. Some "free" accounts do charge.

Other things to look for in a checking account are overdraft protection, the cost of the checks themselves, and the amount charged for stop payments and overdrafts.

Safe Deposit Box

You should definitely have your own safe deposit box if

you have: Savings certificates Stock or bond certificates Insurance policies Deeds Important personal records Will.

The savings, stock and bond certificates, deed and personal records should go in the safe deposit box to prevent theft, loss or damage. Copies of all the above should be kept at home for easy reference and your will and life insurance policy should be kept with your attorney or executor with copies placed in the box and kept at home again for easy reference. Safe deposit boxes are sometimes sealed after death, so that is why your will and life insurance are kept in a more accessible place. Joint ownership of a box only creates problems—make sure you have your own and don't forget where it is. The annual charge runs from about $5 to $25 for small to medium boxes. Some banks offer them free with checking or savings plans.

Your Personal Credit

Today in America your credit is one of your most valuable assets. Credit involves everything from credit cards to loans. The typical spending pattern for young Americans involves a large commitment to borrowing whether it be monthly charges or contracts for several years.

The idea of borrowing is to get the use of an item now rather than saving to make the purchase. Starting a family involves many large purchases and the easiest way to get them is through the use of credit. A more mature family will not have to make so many purchases at once and probably will be saving more than they are spending. So a mature family can use extra savings to make purchases as they become necessary or desirable without resorting to high interest consumer credit.

Establishing Good Credit

The basic components of a good credit rating are a steady, reliable source of income, and a record of having managed that income correctly. i.e. (Having made a previous loan and having successfully paid the loan off.) For some loans a lender may require that you have had a previous loan and paid it off. It is not enough for them to know that you have a steady income stream, they must know how well you have managed your spending habits in the past.

Part of having a sparkling credit rating or at least the best you can have, comes from making rational borrowing decisions. Even if the lenders are willing to give you credit, it may be unwise to use it. Don't use credit for, 1. Extravagant purchases, 2. without a reserve fund, 3. if your job is seasonal or has lay-offs, 4. especially don't borrow up to the hilt of your ability to pay or, 5. on the basis of money that you "expect," but are not certain of getting or when you will get it. These uses of credit most often lead to an over extension and may result in real credit problems. An extra cushion of credit over and above a reserve fund is indeed a good thing to have.

A simple rule will help to point out how much credit you can afford ·

Take home pay—	$1000
Less Rent and utilities	$400
Food	$160
Clothing	$80
Equals Spending Money	$640
	1000
	640
	3⟌360

The RULE Divide by 3   120
equals Total monthly credit payments $120

If you feel you have to borrow to "consolidate" your loans or make the payments then you are in trouble. GO DIRECTLY TO A CREDIT COUNSELING SERVICE IN YOUR COMMUNITY, DO NOT PASS A FINANCE COMPANY. The community service agency will help you to unload your debt. They are there to help not to make a new loan.

If you are denied credit then you have the right by law to know why. You should in fact find out why because there may be an error to be corrected. Or if you have adverse information in a credit file you have the right to have that information removed after 7 years, except in the case of a bankruptcy in which case it is 14 years.

Where to Get Credit

Credit is a matter of convenience. It is often easier to charge it or use a retail installment contract to make a purchase rather than pay in cash or wait until you have saved up enough money to pay the full price all at once. Stores and banks offer credit at no cost if you pay when the bill comes due. You can also spread payments over a period or time if you wish usually at a high rate of interest, 1 to 1½% a month or 12 to 18% Annual Percentage Rate. Retail installment contracts are used most often for major purchases such as automobiles, appliances, T.V.'s and stereos. Retail installment contracts have much higher limits on the Annual Percentage Rate allowed by law. The maximums allowed range from 49% to 17% Annual Percentage Rate.

It may be cheaper to charge a major purchase if you are using credit on a charge card rather than signing a separate retail installment contract. For one thing the first month's interest is free on a charge card. Also always ask what the Annual Percentage Rate is and be sure to check it on the contract itself.

The CHEAPEST Credit is at your bank or credit union. If you can arrange a small loan from your bank - not a finance company - then it will probably be worth the time and effort to apply at your bank. Personal, auto, and other loans range from 8.5 to 18.5% at banks with the average being just about 13% Annual Percentage Rate. Finance companies generally charge more as they service higher risk loans.

"Stuff" to Look Out For

Credit is really a fairly simple thing to shop for. The easiest way is just to get on the phone and call to get information for the type of credit you want to compare:

Charge card: banks or particular store

Open credit: doctors, hospitals, etc.

Retail credit: Auto dealer, appliance store, etc.

Small loan: savings institutions, credit union

The way to compare these lending services is to ask for the 1. Annual Percentage Rate, 2. the amount of finance charge, and 3. what your payment would be on a hypothetical loan amount (term of the loan available). Of course, you will want to know if you can qualify for the loan and if loans are available for the type of purchase you want to make.

Do not go to a debt consolidator. Their interest rates are generally on the high side of outrageous.

If you fall behind on payments and are suddenly served a default judgment without notice, call an attorney or go to your community legal services center and get help.

A balloon payment, large final payment, often accompanies low monthly payments. Beware of such tactics as this. The best way to avoid the balloon payment is to make sure your loan is fully amortized, that is equal monthly payments until the loan is paid off.

If you forget or miss a payment, some lenders will slap heavy penalties on or worse, some will require that the entire balance be paid off immediately. If you have used the car you purchased as collateral for the loan and you miss a payment, you may find your car missing sometime. The Supreme Court now requires that you be notified first.

Beware of warranties and disreputable dealers of major purchase items. The best deals are good, dependable merchandise. Often shoddy items are sold with unbelievable financing.

If you cannot qualify for an interest rate under 18% then you most definitely should not use much credit. It is much better to do without than to buy something you cannot afford.

NOTES

Chapter Five

INSURANCE: YOUR PROTECTION

Any insurance policy you purchase is protection for you and your family in the event of an unforseen disaster. Proper insurance protection frees you of financial worries. Health, life, disability, liability, auto, and homeowner's policies provide about as much protection as you can get. The government provides numerous policies through withholding at work and general welfare but these are not adequate for most needs so private policies can supplement these to give you the kind of protection you want.

The numerous companies and types of policies can be confusing if confronted all at once. Without adequately educating yourself about the basics of shopping for insurance you will find yourself in the midst of numerous salesmen. Each will be using unfamiliar terminology that will make it difficult to make a decision. When a salesman calls to explain a particular policy you should be able to take control and ask the questions that allow you to make a decision. This decision will take less time and hassle and will provide you the satisfaction of knowing that you have the policy that suits you best.

Life Insurance

The easiest way to provide instant protection for your family in the event of death is a life insurance policy. Insurance companies would not be in business if it was not for this need of money at such a time. If you already have an adequate source of money - pensions, Social Security, savings -

or if you do not have any dependents in need, then life insurance is not a good investment. It is an excellent source of protection.

The advantages of life insurance are: Relatively low cost for high amount of protection. Tax free nature. Savings and borrowing power are available with some type of policies.

There is no probate court proceeding before beneficiaries receive the distribution.

One of the biggest questions and certainly one you should have answered before talking to any salesman is: How much protection should I get? The rule of thumb is 4 to 5 times your current annual earnings or enough to meet 70% of your current expenditures. To be more precise make a projected budget with new income from all sources and expenses with inflation. Your cash value should be enough to carry on.

Income
Life insurance
Pensions
Annuities
Jobs
Social security
Savings (interest only)
Expenses
    Mortgage (consider a decreasing term policy to pay this off)
Retraining
College
Normal budget
Other debt
Immediate expenses

Term Insurance

This is the cheapest policy. It provides cash in the event of death for a stated premium (payment) amount for a certain number of years of coverage. It only pays in the event of death. There is no savings or borrowing feature in this policy. Get a renewable policy to avoid having to qualify under another medical exam.

Straight Life

Straight life, ordinary life, and whole life are one and the same name for a policy of life insurance that provides the protection. The policy accumulates a cash value which you can borrow against in an emergency. For many it is "the" way to have a savings account. Of course, this feature does cost more. The same protection with a better return on savings can be had by combining a term policy with an annuity.

Limited Payment Life

Limited payment life is a straight life policy with a certain number of years designated as the years of payment. It gives the same lifetime protection and other features of straight life.

Endowment

This policy stresses the savings aspect of the policy. Cash value builds up quickly. The payments usually are highest under this kind of policy.

Annuities

Annuities are not a form of life insurance at all but are often sold with term policies to form a sort of straight life policy at a cheaper price. The savings feature in a straight life policy will most often be more expensive than an annuity. Annuities provide a fixed monthly payment for life or a certain term according to how much money you have to put in. Annuities are not the answer to retirement because the income is fixed and even moderate inflation will knock a big loop in any fixed income program but an annuity is a good base to work from.

Agents and Companies

Agents are the people who sell the insurance. They represent a company. The most experienced agents carry the designation CLU (Chartered Life Underwriter). Try to deal with these people as they are the most knowledgeable. Also check your library for a copy of their life insurance book to compare policies and prices. Cheaper prices are associated with better companies but be sure your coverage is complete.

Health Insurance

The modern medical bill that supports a high technology medical industry can stagger most any budget. A few days in the hospital for surgery or illness can cost thousands of dollars. If you have to reckon with such a bill could you or would you want to today? The various health insurance and medical plans that are available today are designed to prevent such occurrences. Check with your employer to find out what coverage you have. Many employer health insurance programs are sufficient. Talk to several reputable agents to find out if the coverage with your current insurance is adequate for you and your family. Hospital costs can increase significantly in one or two years.

Hospital Insurance

This form of policy covers expenses while in the hospital. As with most plans the limits and deductibles vary. Some plans pay a fixed amount which in several years may provide enough coverage. The economical type is one that pays a percentage, usually 80% of the bill.

Major Medical Coverage

Major medical policies cover everything (check the policy for exceptions) in the way of medical bills with the policy holder, you, paying a percentage of the bill and a deductible. This type of policy is good extra coverage for other policies that may be weak.

Coverage for Surgery

There are policies for surgery only or cancer only. These types are meant as a supplement to existing programs of insurance you may have rather than as a program in and of itself.

Disability Insurance

Disability insurance covers your loss of income if you are out of commission temporarily or even permanently. Government programs in all probability will not provide enough income to get along on in the event of an illness or injury that extends itself over a long period of time.

Tips on Health Insurance

Buy your insurance through a group for big savings. Unions, employers, associations, clubs, etc. offer policies at group rates, often without a physical.

Mail order health insurance is not a good value and should not generally be purchased even as a supplement.

Be sure your coverage is as complete as you can get. Often exceptions to the policy or limitations are just the sort of thing that may present a high risk to you.

Duplicate coverage often will not pay for a claim. The exceptions are mail order plans that pay to you directly. But their coverage costs more than regular coverage. Do not try to make a profit on your medical problems.

Group medical coverages such as Blue Cross or Blue Shield, provide a full range of services for policy holders and because of their size are generally cheaper.

Check with your doctor's bookkeeper to see which companies pay the best. Doctors may ask you to pay first if the company takes a long time to pay it's claim. You can save a lot of time and hassle if you check this matter out first.

If you cannot afford full coverage a major medical and disability policy are the most important. Use a high deductible for the major medical. If you are out of work because of a disability, and it can happen to the best of us, you will need income. Government policies are just not enough.

HMO - Health Maintenance Organizations

A HMO is a health maintenance system. You can join one or get together with others in your community to form a HMO. Fees are paid at a low rate for care of certain illnesses and preventive care. The services usually range over all the most common problems with exceptions being rare or particularly expensive care for which you would take out a catastrophic illness policy with a high deductible but with a high ceiling coverage.

The federal government in 1973 enacted a law to encourage the development and use of HMO. The Kaiser Permanente plan is the prototype for HMO's. It is interesting to note that through the Kaiser plan use of preventive medical care (HMO) the number of patients needing hospital care is about one half of some Blue Cross plans.

Auto Insurance

All states require that you have automobile insurance to protect you and others on the road. To get the best protection buy as much insurance as you can afford. The following are the major risk categories that you need protection for.
Liability - Covers you for accidents in which death or injury results. Get as much coverage as you can afford. It is a very small increase in cost for high protection.
Property damage - Covers claims against you if you damage other's property including cars, utility poles, houses, etc.
Medical payments - Pays medical expenses regardless of who is at fault.
Comprehensive - Repairs your car in case of any events except collision.

Collision - Repairs your car in the event that it is involved in a collision.
Uninsured motorist - Protects against damages due to an accident with an uninsured motorist or a hit and run.

Most policies cover you if you are driving someone else's car with permission or you let someone else drive your car with permission.

To find what company has the lowest rates simply find out what coverage you need and call several, at least six, to see what the total cost of a policy would be for you.

Cutting the Cost of an Auto Policy

Check to see if you are eligible for a group policy at work or through an organization you belong to.

Do not buy a policy from the dealer who sold you the car - most such policies are very expensive.

If you move to a new area check to see what the rates are in your new area. The rates vary considerably from suburb to city with cities generally having a higher rate.

Many people recommend cutting insurance cost by upping the deductible to $250 to $500. Do not do this if it would destroy your budget to have to pay the deductible.

No Fault Insurance

No fault insurance is offered in many states. It's main benefit is that you are paid whether you are at fault or not.

The big problem is that no fault restricts your right to sue for injuries sustained in auto accidents. Essentially the state sets up minimum payment amounts for injuries and loss of wages. Even if your injury costs more, your right to sue is restricted.

Homeowner Insurance

Standard policy forms are available through most agents. Forms 1, 2, 3 and 5 cover damage to your house or belongings. Some provide additional payments if you are forced to live in temporary quarters after a mishap. Form 1 provides the most basic coverage, with forms 3 and 5 providing progressively better coverage for the homeowners home and personal liability responsibilities.

To reduce the cost of a policy increase your deductibles but only if you can afford to pay off the deductible. Be sure to update your policy frequently. Yearly updates are about right with the costs of building increasing so rapidly. Condominium owners use a form 6 for coverage not included in the policies used by the owner's association.

Most policies cover the contents of your home so make a list and take photos of your home contents. Keep it in a safety deposit box for safe keeping. If you have unusually valuable or rare items have them appraised and get extra coverage for these items. If you cannot get private coverage for your valuables most states offer a federally subsidized insurance.

Your personal liability can be increased considerably for a very small cost. You should have as much of this coverage as is reasonable.

Do shop different companies for your homeowner's needs as rates will vary considerably. Be sure you are comparing similar coverages.

Tenants Insurance

If you are a renter you need form 4 (mentioned above) to cover yourself for personal property and emergency living expenses. Be sure you get personal liability coverage. You may be charged with damages to the apartment caused by your neglect. Check with your landlord to see if you need this damages coverage or if the landlord's coverage will be enough.

Social Security

The government has set up under the Social Security Act of 1935 and amendments to that act programs for retirement, disability, survivors, and medical aid (Medicare). Before these programs everyone had to rely on private programs and/or relatives in a time of need. If you did not have any of these advantages you were simply out of luck. Today over 90% of employees have the benefits of these government insurance programs. Although these programs are not an end-all they do provide substancial benefits.

To be eligible for these programs you must have a job or be a dependent of someone who does. The amount of time you must work to be eligible varies so if you are not quite sure whether you are eligible for benefits and you find yourself in need, call your local Social Security office (Under United States Government in the white pages) and tell them your position and ask if there is any benefit available to you. You do not automatically start receiving checks when you retire, become disabled, need medical care or someone who supports you dies. The programs require that you apply for the benefits to receive them.

Retirement Benefits

Retirement benefits of the Social Security program are paid to retirees. If you retire at age 65 you will receive the full benefits entitled to you, after you apply of course. If you retire at age 62 you will receive monthly checks of about 80% of the amount you would receive if you had waited until age 65. It is possible to retire even earlier but those checks will be even less than the 80%.

To find out just how much benefit you are eligible for when you retire consult the local office of the Social Security Administration. The amount changes with the Consumer Price Index (CPI) and is based on your earnings over the years. If the CPI increases 3% or more in any one year the benefit amount is increased by that percentage. You can increase your benefits if you work after you retire. Be careful though about how much you are making because if you earn too much, approximately $2,760 per year; benefits will be reduced $1 for each $2 that is earned. This rule applies to everyone under the age of 72. If you are over 72 you can go to work and make all the money you want without having your Social Security retirement check reduced at all. Let me stress that Social Security checks should not be your sole source of money when you retire. (See Chapter on Financial Passages).

Spouses are also entitled to Social Security retirement benefits. Your spouse may collect on his/her own earnings or it may benefit your spouse more to collect as your spouse under a joint Social Security account. Spouses can make independent decisions regarding retirement. If your spouse wants to retire at 62 he/she can and still receive 36% of the full benefit amount. If your spouse waits until age 65 the amount becomes 50% of your full benefit amount.

Dependent children are entitled to benefits under the Act. If you have dependent children your benefit amount will be larger. Dependents may be claimed by either husband's or wives accounts.

This last changes frequently regarding benefits and eligibility. If you have any questions after this brief review please get in touch with your local Social Security office.

Disability

Eligible employees or self employed persons may apply for and receive disability benefits under the Social Security Act. If you are under age 65 and become disabled and think that you will be so disabled for the next 12 months or more or if your disability will result in death then you are eligible for benefits under the disability program. The program pays benefits in much the same way as you would be paid under the retirement program.

Survivors Program

The Survivors program is similar to term insurance in that eligible worker's families receive money at the time of the worker's death. To be eligible the family must have children. Sole surviving spouses do not get any benefit until age 60 when normal retirement benefits are allowed. A spouse caring for dependent children is entitled to a benefit. Dependent children to age 18 or to age 22 if full time student receive monthly benefit checks from the Social Security Administration.

Medicare

Medicare is another program in the Social Security Administration. You may be eligible for Medicare if you are over age 65, have a kidney disease, or are disabled at any age. Briefly the Medicare program comes in two parts: A and B. Part A covers you if you are covered under the retirement program or you can voluntarily get coverage if you apply and pay a modest premium. Part B is voluntary and is recommended as it supplies generous coverage at low rates.

Part A for eligible individuals covers in part or whole 90 days in a hospital (60 days extra lifetime reserve). There is a deductible of $124 but almost all hospital bills are covered.

Part B has a $60 deductible that you have to pay against excellent coverage for medical expenses outside a hospital. Physicians services, outside a hospital, outpatient services, X-rays, and physical therapy are covered under Part B. Remember, Part B is voluntary and you must pay a nominal amount for the coverage but it is well worth it. If you want, when you become eligible to sign up, the premium increases 10% a year.

Anyone who has a certain kidney problem or who has been receiving Social Security disability benefits for 24 months is eligible. The benefits are the same as Part A and Part B above. Call your Social Security Office for more information.

Medicaid

Medicaid is medical care for low income, disabled, or blind people. The program provides hospital, doctor and therapy services and is funded jointly by the federal government and states. Additional dental care, prescription drugs, glasses and check ups are available through the Program. You need not be old to collect Medicaid - just in need. Medicaid can be applied against Medicare deductibles if you qualify for both. The plan is administered by the state and local welfare agencies. To get more information, call or write your welfare department.

Food Stamps

Food stamps are federal assistance to those in need administered through local welfare offices. If you are hungry and do not have enough money to buy some food then you should apply at your welfare office for food stamps. Food stamps are not used to mail food just to buy food. Low income people (including students), no income people, Social Security, or welfare recipients are eligible for food stamps benefits.

Worker's Compensation
(formerly Workman's Compensation)

You are covered under the Worker's Compensation program if you work in one of the 50 states for an employer who is required to participate in the program. Most large firms are covered but if you are self employed, work for a small firm, are a seasonal worker, or think your employer is flaky, then check it out with the local Worker's Compensation office to find out if you are covered. Coverage in this case means being reimbursed for loss of wages and medical expenses (some limits) in the event you are injured on the job only.

NOTES

Chapter Six

INVESTING FOR TOMORROW'S MONEY

Making an investment is just another step in your plan for personal money management. Your budget contains a section for savings and investment to provide money in the future for some specific purpose. When you have enough liquid (easily convertible to cash) savings, you will undoubtedly have future goals to achieve in the way of financial achievements. You may want a boat, camper, or big vacation and you will need to consider your retirement years' income. The great majority of us do not plan adequately nor take enough action to achieve realistic goals for retirement income. Inflation, being what it is, takes the biggest chunk out of future plans. (See Financial Passages Chapter). A good investment program will hedge your investments against the dangers of inflation.

A larger return than a savings account or US treasury bills requires that you take some risk. U.S. treasury bills are considered the safe rate or zero risk. However, these means of investing seldom provide much real return on the dollar. In other words you are merely preserving your dollar's earning power in the face of inflation and in some years you may have lost money in terms of inflation.

Inflation is measured by government statistics. If your savings are earning 7% in a time deposit, in all probability your dollars are just keeping equal purchasing power. Some luxury type items prices are increasing at fantastically higher rates.

Investment Requirements

Earning more than 7%, the safe rate, means that you must invest in investment that contains some risk. The higher the risk, the higher the return you will demand. Some will be too risky for you and some may not provide the return you want for the associated risk. The means of reducing risk and increasing returns is through knowledge. The informed investor is not sold any investment - he simply orders a purchase (after doing the research). The knowledgeable investor will evaluate the many investment alternatives in relation to a set of desired goals:

1. Amount of return desired (growth of dollars).

2. Amount of risk to be allowed (preservation of dollars).

3. Amount of time available; for analysis of investment, for management of investment.

Another goal to consider is the amount of sleep you can get under various investment alternatives. Some people can sleep well with the most speculative, risky investment while others will not rest unless their money is safe in a safe.

The following is a list of various investment vehicles. Some will suit you and no doubt many will not suit you. For some risk will be too high, for others the time will present a constraint, and yet others returns may not be sufficient to justify an investment for you.

Passbook savings	Time account savings
Treasury bills	US saving Bonds
Stock	Preferred Stock
Short sales of stock	Puts and Call options
Bonds	Funds
Commodities	Residential Real Estate
Commercial Real Estate	Land
Real Estate syndicates	Real estate investment trust (REITs)
Annuities	Commodity futures
Antiques, Art, Stamps, Coins	

Stocks

Stock is far and away the most common of all investments available today. You can get in with the smallest amount and come out with the greatest. Everybody has feelings about the stock market. Its either up or down, or I made money or I lost money. People become very emotional when speaking of the stock market, yet they shouldn't because investment in the stock of a company is a logical, cold decision. If you do become emotional about your stock investment decisions you may very well pay for it.

The only way to make money in the market is to do research. Research will enlighten you to the point where when you go to your stock broker you tell your broker what you want. You may pick a very competent broker who will give you good leads but your leads should be checked out by you for the quality of the stock as well as how well the stock fits into your investment criteria, i.e. do you have to watch it everyday or can you just check it occasionally? Do you want to check it everyday?

114

Typically stock investment returns are greater than those of savings institutions. Of course the risk associated with stock is much greater than saving so if you invest in stock you can minimize your risk by getting a good understanding of the market and it's mechanisms. The local library will undoubtedly have a number of primer books to get your wheels rolling in the terminology and concepts of the market. The large brokerage houses provide voluminous literature on individual stock as well as the market and the economy.

I recommend the "Value Line Investment Survey" for information regarding stock listed on the New York Stock Exchange. The financial section of large metropolitan newspapers will help you to keep up with daily economic and market information as well as significant events regarding particular companies. Many of the larger banks also provide significant economic forecasts in the way of a brief annual or monthly report. Information is your most important assest.

Stock Trading

You can buy stock from anyone but the largest volume of trading occurs on the organized exchanges or through your broker. The New York Stock Exchange (NYSE) is the biggest. All company stock traded on the NYSE must meet certain financial requirements. The American Stock Exchange (Amex) also has financial requirements for listed stock however the requirements are somewhat less stringent. The Over-the-Counter (OTC) market is a less than formally organized market where brokers deal directly between themselves. The National Association of Securities Dealers (NASD) now has an automatic quote system to provide quotes for members. OTC stock is generally of smaller, newer companies, and are traded less frequently.

If you do not know anyone with the stock you want to buy (most people don't) then you will want to choose a broker to make your transaction for you. You will again have to enter the market place to shop for a broker who provides the services you want at the price you want. Generally if you are a beginner you will want to stick with a large reputable firm. Ask for someone who specializes in the area you are interested in. Talk to several firms and compare prices as you will find that commission schedules vary depending on the service and amount of research you get.

Blue Chip, Glamour, Income Stock Etc.

Two major stock types are common and preferred stock. Preferred stock is always called preferred stock. It is called preferred stock because this stock has a first claim on dividend distribution. Common stock types are:

Blue chip — A low risk, well established company with long term safety.

Speculative stock — High risk stock

Defensive stock — A stock not sensitive to recession.

Cyclical stock — A stock that rises and falls with the economy.

Income stock — A stock that has provided a consistent, regular, dividend

Growth — A stock whose sales and earnings are dramatically increasing.

Glamour Stock — A well publicized growth stock or stock of a publicized industry.

Tips for Investing

Don't invest more than you can afford to lose in a speculative stock.

Time your investments. Try to buy at market bottoms and sell at market tops.

Develop a strategy for buying, holding stock.

Do not wait for a loser to come back to your price. If it drops a certain percentage—sell. You can always buy again.

Take a profit when you have made it.

Buy on fundamentals. That is, buy on growth in sales, earnings, dividends, etc.

Thoroughly check out new issues. Read the prospectus for important clues to a company's vitality.

Keep abreast of news affecting your stock or potential stock.

Always read the annual report from the company.

For long term investment pick a company that leads its industry in an economicaly sound industry.

Stock Options

Stock options are a specialized method of investing in stock. Options are either puts or calls and may be either written or bought. A call is an option to buy a stock at a given price. A put is an option to sell a stock at a certain price. If you own a stock that you think will decline in value you may want to write a call at the peak price and sell it. You will be placing your money on the belief that the stock will decline in value. If it does decline, you have received the money for the

117

call. If it increases you have received the call money and will have to deliver the stock you optioned at the option price. Options are a sophisticated investment tool.

Short Sales

A short sale of stock is a sale of stock you do not own. You borrow a hundred shares of stock and sell them. Then later you will have to purchase the stock (hopefully at a lower price than you sold them for) and repay your "loan". Short sales have a higher risk than a regular purchase because if the stock goes up there is no limit to what you might have to pay when you finally have to make the purchase.

Buy "On the Margin"

Your broker may allow you to borrow money to buy stock. This is called buying on the margin. Margin buying gives the buyer a higher risk component because he must: 1.) pay interest on the borrowed money and 2.) increases or decreases in value of a stock are magnified.

Regular		
Buy Jan 1 100 shares x $50/share =	$5,000	cash
sell Jan 1 100 shares x $55/share =	$5,500	
Profit	500	
% of Profit on cash =	10%	
Margin		
Buy Jan 1 100 shares x $50/share =	$5,000	
Jan 1 Borrow $2,500	$2,500	
Investment	$2,500	(cash)
Sell Jan 10 at $55	$5,500	Profit
Profit	500	
% Profit on cash	20%	

Margin accounts are regulated by law and broker's requirements regarding your financial position.

Bonds

A bond is a debt instrument of a corporation. Bonds are usually issued in $1,000 denominations and pay interest to the holder of the bonds. Owing to the size of each individual bond it is not feasible to invest in bonds unless you buy about ten at one time. The transaction costs of buying and selling the bonds do not make it a viable investment for the small investor unless you buy in a mutual fund that buys bonds. Mutual fund shares sell on the stock market. (See Mutual Funds.)

Currently bonds pay a higher rate of interest than savings accounts. So why not invest in bonds rather than save? For one thing, the price of a bond will vary with money market interest rates. For another, the investment in bonds is somewhat speculative. There is no federal guarantee that you will get your money back if the company goes under. Also, bonds vary in quality and type so it is important that you be familiar with the differences between one bond issue and another.

If you decide that you want to buy corporate bonds be sure you do your research. Then find a broker (most stock brokerage houses handle bonds) who will take the time to analyze your particular situation. Check the commission schedules as small purchases may have a prohibitively high commission.

Tax Free Municipals

Municipal bonds are issued by cities and states to finance education, highways and you name it. Until the now famous New York City monetary crisis most municipal bonds were thought to be of the highest quality of municipal bonds.

As with corporate bonds the maturity is usually at least five years with most becoming due in twenty years. Serial bonds refer to issues that are paid off in groups by serial number so that the full value does not become due all at once.

The tax free aspect of these bonds makes them most interesting to the high tax bracket investor. The federal government does not tax these bonds and in some states bonds from within the state are also tax free. A yield is the percent of income you receive per year on your purchase of bonds.

Tax Bracket	Municipal bond Yield	Equals Tax Free Yield
30%	5%	7.14%
40	5%	8.33%
50	5%	10.00%

Government Bonds

US government bonds like municipals or corporate bonds are risk free and are not marketable except back to the government. Treasury bills are issued by the government with short term maturities and are very marketable. Since they are marketable before maturity they are sensitive to interest rate fluctuations and I do not recommend T-bills unless you can hold them to maturity, usually three to six months.

US Savings Bonds are a unique risk free means of saving. If you are the type who saves for six months then you end up spending your savings, US savings bonds may be good for your budget. Many large employers and banks have plans that allow you to put so much per week or month directly into US Savings Bonds.

The bonds are liquid in that in an emergency you can present them for collection at the Federal Reserve Bank or for E bonds at your local bank. There are some time restrictions and if you cash in before maturity the yield is very low. Currently at maturity series E and H bonds yield 6%. Not a bad way to save.

E and H bonds are the most popular bond types. These bonds are exempt from state and local taxes. The interest income on E bonds may be deferred until the bond matures in five years. If you continue to invest the interest in E bonds the interest income remains deferred from your taxes. H bonds mature in 10 years and pay interest checks semi-annually.

US saving bonds are a good place to invest some of your money and they are an excellent place to begin a savings program if you have trouble retaining your savings.

Mutual Funds

A mutual fund is a pooling together of money to buy stocks, bonds, and other investments. Shares of these funds sell on the organized exchanges and prices are listed in the financial section of your newspaper. A mutual fund will buy shares of many different companies. Most funds specialize in particular type of stock (growth income, etc.) or industry electronics, utilities, bonds, etc.

Funds may be load or no load and open end or closed end. Load fund means that it costs you a commission to buy. You can calculate the commission by subtracting the bid from the Net Asset Value (NAV) from the offering price and dividing the NAV.

$$\frac{\text{Offer Price—NAV}}{\text{NAV}} = \% \text{ commission}$$

The commissions are rather hefty as you will see. Load funds are available from brokers while no-load funds are available from the fund itself with no commission charge. NO-load funds perform just as well if not better than load funds—you just have to shop a little more to get one.

Mutual funds are a good investment for investor's with little expertise and money. Make a determination of the kind of fund you want and check performance in the business periodicals.

Commodities

Commodities are soybeans, grains, wood, metal, and money. Trading is conducted in organized markets for spot (present delivery) and futures (future delivery). Almost all trading is done on narrow margin contract.

Wheat Contract

Wheat 5,000 bushels ¼¢/bushel min. move = $12.50 contract
Jan 1 buy 5,000 bu x $3.30/bu =
      $16,500 on 10% margin = $1650 cash
Jan 10 sell 5,000 bu x $3.00/bu = 15,000
                                   1,500
commission   45
cash loss   1,545
cash $105 = 94% loss of
                                              cash

As you can see it does not take much of a move to get wiped out in highly leverage commodities. Prices fluctuate according to supply and demand factors. Supply is affected by plantings, growing season weather, and blight. Demand is affected by world supply, domestic use, and overseas purchases. Price is also affected by anticipation of these factors. Do not speculate in commodities unless you are wealthy and well informed.

Oil and Gas Shelters

The government has sponsored through tax shelters private exploration for oil and gas reserves. Individuals may participate in these high risk ventures. If you do investigate these speculative ventures to shelter your capital be sure that 1.) more than one oil company is investing. 2.) promotors are not paid unless oil is struck and 3.) that you know wildcat drilling is even riskier.

Annuities

Annuities are contracts where you pay a life insurance company a specified amount of money per month or year and

123

in return they will return your money plus interest. If you are thinking "ahha-fixed income for life" you better think twice. Fixed is the catch—with inflation a fixed amount is really a decreasing amount. (See page 150 and Money Book No. 7 page 87)

Don't let me sell annuities short. They are an excellent way to save tax deferred dollars for a very nice nest egg. As a matter of fact it is a good place to begin your retirement program.

Real Estate Investment

Real Estate is one of those investments that you have to save for to get but that once you get it and do it well it all seems worthwhile. Real estate as an investment requires time, a large initial investment, and an income or cash reserve. You operate a real estate investment like a business. Time is required to investigate and become knowledgeable about the particular market you enter. Real estate for the most part requires a large downpayment and financing with a loan. The downpayment may be 20% or 50% but because real estate properties are such large investments this 20% may easily be $10,000. Since the typical real estate investment is heavily financed, the lender will require that you have an adequate income to maintain the property.

The many different methods of investing in and types of real estate make real estate a large field for investment. You should pick the type of investment that fits in with your budget, investment strategy, and time requirements. Although lending institutions do a very thorough job of making sure that any real estate investment fits in with your budget, it is possible for you to get a loan on real estate that may be more than you should take. Creative financing is such a way that a lender has no control over your obtaining a loan or future changes in your household income are ways to get around a lender's borrowing requirements that may lead to trouble if you are not realistic enough to plan thoroughly for the life of the investment under the various possible circumstances. I recommend that you keep a special cash reserve of from 4 months to one year depending on the strength of your income.

Investment strategy is a means of determining what you want to put into real estate and what you want to get out. It involves a studying of the relevant literature and discussing your goals and constraints with qualified investment counselors to come up with a plan. Your plan should include plans for the following topics:

Initial Investment: budget money, time for investigation

Type of investment: land, income property, time required for investment to pay off

Goal: Amount of return (dollars), amount of time (personal time)

Land

Although land is the easiest investment, timewise, to maintain, it requires considerable investigation up front. Land is largely paid for in cash with maximum financing of up to 50%. Land may be classified as an alligator for investment purposes. That is it eats—taxes, interest, and assessments. The long term trend for land is up.

If you want to buy land as a hedge against inflation, which indeed it has been over the years, you will want to get a "good deal" on your land. To get a good deal you can either luck out or take some time to study what makes land grow in value.

How to Invest in Land

1. Read books about real estate and land investments.

2. Talk to neighbors, friends, associates professionals, and Realtors about land in your area.

3. Become aware of city, county, and regional plans and patterns of expansion.

4. Acquaint yourself with zoning codes.

5. Keep abreast of new developments in planning and economics in your area.

6. Find the parcel that suits you and the next buyer and the eventual user.

Residential Income Property

Residential income property requires more time in management than land but it is usually not such an alligator. The income from your units will pay for the taxes, interest, and maintenance. I say usually because in areas of high appreciation property values have out distanced increases in rent and anticipation of rent increases.

Residential income property may be single family residences, duplexes, or apartment buildings. The amount of rent you receive in proportion to value increases with the number of units in a particular parcel. The amount of time and money spent maintaining an investment will increase with age. Older buildings will require replacement of various appliances, carpets, (deferred maintenance) etc. When you buy your building you will want to compare these various features to see how much additional investment is necessary to bring the building up to par. If you want to spend a minimum of time with your investment you will want to look for a building that is new and does not require much maintenance.

Being a first time investor you may want to consider a "fixer" for your investment. These are buildings that require a bit of deferred maintenance and their price will reflect this. If you know what it costs to fix up a building or you are skilled at it yourself you can buy a fixer and make the needed repairs and sell the now beautiful building for a quick profit. The important thing about fixers and quick profit is to know value:

Fixer duplex cost		$34,000
Closing cost		600
Fixing expense		500
Total Cost		$35,100
Value when renovated		$42,000
less: Total Cost	35,100	
cost of sale	2,900	
	38,000	
PROFIT	$4,000	

Profit

The above illustrates the possibility associated with a fixer in poor condition and the profit from fixing it up for an investor who wants no problems with an investment. Be sure that you know values or you may be sinking fix up expense into an investment that will just pay for itself with no profit for your work and management.

If you buy income property your income from the property will be dependent on the rent the property commands. In comparing values of property you will find that most are valued based on their income from rents. So it is therefore important that you are just as familiar with rents in the area you invest in as property values. Many real estate sales salespeople will tell that the "rents are low". When you get to the point of making the decision you should know whether the rents are high or low. Sometimes an owner will raise rents as the proper economic rent.

Value is determined by three methods and then reconciled. Income approach—Bases value on the amount of income less standard and applicable expenses.

Market comparison—Bases value on the comparison of sales of similar property with adjustments for any differences.

Replacement cost—The upper limit of value is the land cost plus costs of developing a new structure minus depreciation. How to Invest In Residential Income Property:

1. Follow the steps in How to Budget in Land as applied to apartments.

2. Join an apartment owners association in your community and utilize their services.

3. Check out the possibility of rent control for your locality.

4. Become an expert in apartment values or if you cannot do this, order a professional appraisal of your potential purchase.

Commercial and Industrial Real Estate Investment

Commercial properties, industrial, retail, and office buildings are for the experienced expert. I advise anyone who is not such a person to stick to more conventional investments.

Syndicates, Partnerships, and REIT's

Multiple ownership of real estate is a means to acquire larger, more sophisticated properties. To some, I would say yes and some no. Generally, if the promoters come to you directly I would be extra wary. Promoters are often paid whether the project makes money or not. You can almost be sure that a promoter will take extra care in choosing an investment if his being paid is contingent on the investment's success.

Another item in organizations where you do not have control of management is that you will pay for management. One organization I looked at recently had the following fees: 60%. That means for every dollar "invested" only 40% was used as a down payment on the property. Furthermore their prospectus did not include prospective properties for evaluation and the company was considering development of new buildings a highly speculative venture. What's really funny is that I listened to a promoter with a "free" breakfast. It seemed like a good buy until I read the prospectus.

The more people you have in a partnership the more opinions there are—the more differences of opinion. If you are asked to "go in" on partnership consider, 1. who is operating the show and how they are paid. 2. who the other partners you are into the business with are, 3. what control you have over your investment, and 4. having a CPA and/or an attorney who specializes in real estate partnership investments give you an opinion as to the viability of the prospective investment.

REIT's or Real Estate Investment Trusts are corporations whose stock is traded that you may invest in a more conventional manner. Basically there are two types of trusts, mortgage trusts and investment trusts. The mortgage trusts primarily put their money into mortgages and investments, trusts into equity positions. Perhaps you heard that many REIT's went belly up in the mid to early seventies. It is true but now some have regained their foothold and may be a good investment. As with any investment be knowledgeable and pick the investment from the top of the field.

Other Investments

The other investments that are available to you are really more specialized hobbies where profit comes with years and years of experience. If you are willing to take up an investment hobby you will find that there is a great deal of enjoyment to be found in becoming an expert. The most popular and profitable (for the knowledgeable) hobbies are:
Stamps—Coins—Art—Books—Diamonds—Antiques

Stamp collecting is generally considered a hobby. For most it is but some invest in the most rare stamps for appreciation. The largest appreciation occurs in the most expensive stamps. You should specialize in a particular type of stamp—be it airmail, British or early American. Find a reputable dealer—not all are.

Coins are much like stamps in that the most rare, ancient, mint condition coins are the best investment. Proper storage is necessary for any type of collection. Check with your dealer for the proper means of storing your coins.

Art is another hedge against inflation for the wealthy or extravagant speculator. In this particular field very special knowledge is required. Since the field is so diversified from sculpture, to oil to prints, it is very important to find a field you have particular interest in. Take courses in art history—find out what makes the works of the masters such as Picasso so great. Community colleges offer art appreciation programs that will give you the basics. Attending auctions that you can find out about at the local gallery will give you insights to pricing valuable work.

Books—Rare manuscripts are a really unbelievable investment. Rennaisance era, illuminated bibles from Europe sell for hundreds of thousands of dollars. The finest, most rare work will gain the most in appreciation over the years. If you have a rare book or think you have, do NOT get it rebound or change anything about it. Original works in the original covers are worth quite a bit more than a manuscript that has been "fixed".

Diamonds—Diamonds are another big time investment. Minimum investment quality diamonds should be valued at $10,000 wholesale. Since most of us are not dealers and dealers mark up diamonds for sale 40% to 200%, it is hard to strike a bargain. That is you buy at retail prices and sell at wholesale—it takes some heavy appreciation over many years to close the gap and make the investment profitable.

Antiques—How does one tell if an antique is genuine? Only if the origin and manufacturer are identifiable can you tell. For the most part, investing in antiques is risky because as styles change so do values. So if you are shopping for antiques, shop for something practical that you can use and maybe you will have the luck to pick an item that will be a classic. Auctions provide the best bargains as prices are less than retail.

NOTES

Chapter Seven

THE FINANCIAL FACTS OF LIFE

Over the years of your life you will do many things and many things will happen to you. Many of these things will cost you or make you money. That is what this chapter is about—every major event in your lifetime (not heretofore mentioned) that will cause you to pull out your wallet or check book to make a major expenditure.

You should be aware of these expenditures in planning your budget. Like the Boy Scouts say "Be prepared". It sure helps to have the money when the time comes.

One of the major thrusts of this chapter is to acquaint you with the financial events that may happen during your lifetime and not only to acquaint you but to urge you to learn how to get the most for your money. Admittedly, these times of your life will be very emotional but if you think and write down a plan far enough in advance for each expenditure, it will be much easier to deal with when the time comes. And often it's here before you know it—so at least take some time now to discuss these important events in light of the comments I have to make and put a place in your budget for each item (a convenient reminder for when the time comes).

Birth and Young People

Babies are a wonderful thing to have—under the proper circumstances. As far as this book is concerned the proper circumstances involve your financial ability to bear the costs of bringing a young person into the world and then raising the young person without throwing away your budget.

Of course, the proper way to do anything is to plan. To plan for a birth and subsequent child you must know what expenses are involved. The following is a list of expenses that you will have to navigate through upon your decision to bring a young person into this world. Obstetrician—during pregnancy through birth (usually a fixed fee)

Maternity wardrobe	Circumcision fee
Babies school for parents	Pediatrician fee-for the baby
Hospital care	Other special Practical care -nurse at home
Daily charge	Baby's wardrobe
Nursery room	Baby's nursery
Delivery charge	

How do you cut these costs that can easily run $2,000? Shop for your services, get only what you need, and accept gifts. The largest costs are in order:
Hospital care
Obstetrician
Baby's wardrobe & nursery

So start at the middle. Find an obstetrician you like and trust by asking friends and acquaintances whom you respect for names of obstetricians who they found were qualified and reasonable. Try to choose your obstetrician in an area that is conveniently located for you.

The reason I say start at the middle is that not all obstetricians can work at all hospitals. The next order of business is to make an appointment with the obstetrician you have decided to try.

135

While you are making your appointment casually ask the nurse what the doctor charges and at what hospital he works. After you get answers to these questions you may want to cancel your appointment but if the doctor's fee is reasonable and the hospital is reasonable and modern then you will actually want to make the appointment. At this appointment try to evaluate your doctor to be sure you will get along; this is important. If you feel you will not get along you will have to find another obstetrician.

During the birth and for sometime there after you, the mother, will find it difficult to find a job. Unless you hire a nurse or send your child to pre-school nursery you will be quite occupied. Of course, after you have your baby it is too late to consider your work unless you are skilled enough to make money to pay for child care while you are at work, or unless your husband would kindly consent to doing the child raising.

Adoption of a young person may be the way you bring a son or daughter into your home to love and adore. If you do try to adopt a young person you will find it is not that easy. You must qualify financially, have references, and wait, usually one heck of a long time. The nice thing about it is that most state agencies are free of charge. The private licensed agencies will however, charge a fee that varies from a standard $1,000 to $1,500 to exorbitant amounts and black market adoptions are very, very expensive, risky and not recommended.

If you already have a houseful of young people or you are not inclined to raising young people at this time, numerous birth control clinics and devices are available to prospective birth controllers. Planned Parenthood is probably the best place to seek advice about your strategy. It may be noted of course that "An ounce of prevention is worth a pound of cure" and this applies in terms of money as well as emotional terms. When you decide that you have reached the upper limits of reproduction, sterilization is a fairly safe birth control procedure that is relatively cheap and effective. Two things about sterilization that you should be aware of though. 1. It requires about $150 for men and $500 for women. 2. It is for all practical purposes permanent.

If it is too late and you are pregnant and you have decided that it is your choice not to go ahead with the pregnancy you should seek the counsel of the Planned Parenthood organization and a qualified physician, as soon as possible. The first three months are the time when it is easiest to have an abortion. If you wait longer than that, it will cost more and there is higher probability of complications. An abortion during the first three months should cost about $150 and after that the cost is higher, from $400 and more.

The Ins and Outs of Education

It costs a lot to go to college and the costs of education will continue to rise in the future. But so many jobs today require a college degree and or specialized training that in all probability you will have to include a space in the old budget for educational expense. Even if you do not use a college degree for getting a job it is nice to have an education. A really good education gives you the power to see just how really screwed up the world is and more importantly it gives you the necessary tools to screw it up even more. Seriously though, more and more people are turning to college and continuing education courses to take up an interest, learn a skill, or to make an attempt at grasping what is really happening in this world.

The most expensive item in college is support. Anyone who attends college must also live, eat, sleep, and pay tuition. This paragraph is dedicated to the proposition that a large part of the cost of education can be whittled down with a job. Having a job while attending college means either having a part time job while attending school full time or attending school full time and working part time and vacations. A part time job should bring in at least $40 a week which goes a long way on the typical student budget. Most colleges have a job placement program for students who are attending the school. The best jobs are working at the school or at a job that will prepare you to do the kind of job you want to do when you finish school. Try if at all possible not to get a pump jockey type of job that will lead only to pumping more gas.

The balance of an education can usually be financed through the numerous student loan programs available to the school you plan to attend. Be forewarned that these loans take an incredibly long time to process. If you want your loan to fund before the term is over you should apply at the earliest date that applications are accepted. Not all students are eligible for all loans as loan funds are somewhat limited and those with the most need are served first. Consult with the student loan program people and read the college catalog for information about who qualifies for what kind of and how much loan at your school.

Another method of paying the cost of an education is through scholarships. Scholarships are awarded based on need and previous scholastic performances. To save yourself some time trying to figure out which scholarships you may be eligible for, make a trip to the scholarship office and ask what scholarships are available to you. Most scholarship departments will perform the search for you. If you don't hear from them after a reasonable time, give them a call to be sure your application is still being processed. Also, usually you will have to reapply for scholarships every year.

One of the most important methods of meeting the cost of an education is to cut the costs. Tuition can be dealt with effectively by 1) attending a community college for the first two years, 2) attending a public college. Private college tuition is quite a bit more than public colleges. As far as value is concerned you can always get what you want out of a school by putting a lot in. A really top notch education, though, is more easily attained at a school that specializes in high academic standards. To find such a school talk to educators and friends and check to see what accreditation the college has. Room and board is another major expense where you can save big dollars by just comparing costs at the various dormitories. On any campus you will find a great deal of difference between dorms themselves and also off campus housing with dorms having the biggest savings. Some extra costs to include in living off campus are transportation and extra time in preparing meals that could be used working or studying.

If college education is not the kind of education for you, numerous other means of achieving similar goals are available, some at much lower cost. Community colleges have any number of adult education programs on topics ranging from vocational to hobbies. The cost of these classes is minimal. Universities offer continuing education on business, academic, and cultural levels at a slightly higher cost.

Weddings

It is so easy to go overboard on creating a fabulous wedding to indulge yourself and impress your friends. Be aware that it is possible to have a perfectly nice wedding and not spend $4,000 at the same time. How can I do this and still have a beautiful wedding you ask? Well, check the following list of items that can significantly cut down the chances of going broke while throwing a wedding party.

Ring-It is an easy thing to splurge on a ring so set a limit of what you can spend and shop around for a reputable jeweler who will guarantee the quality of his merchandise. Have the ring periodically checked to be sure that any gems remain properly set.

Honeymoon-If you are planning to travel be sure to book well in advance. Also by planning the wedding at such a time that accommodations will be "off season" you will be able to get a better room at a lower cost.

Reception-Have it at your home if you possibly can. Get a good stereo instead of hiring a band. Have a buffet instead of dinner. Shop for a catering service if you prefer a professional service.

Clothes-Tuxedos can be rented and this is recommended unless you plan to wear your tux frequently. Wedding dress can be made, altered or bought brand new.

Gifts-Buy gifts where the bride has a bridal registry. In this way you can be sure that you are buying something that will be useful. Quality items are best so long as the style will always be in style.

Your Career or How to Make the Most of What You Do

This section is dedicated to the proposition that being aware of your abilities and job potential will get you the highest paying job in your field. Whatever your job from fast food worker to corporate executive, there probably are opportunities doing the same or equivalent job where you can make more money. Why bother to save and shop for the bargains if you are throwing away money at your job? You should be aware of the range of jobs that may be available to you in your field or a related one **and** the pay scale. You should optimize your earnings by working for the best paying company.

All this is not to say that if you hear so-and-so is making 5% or 10% more than you that you should run and immediately apply at so-and-so's company. There may be reasons why the other company pays more. They may want to attract the top talent and if it turns out that you are not top talent, after quitting your job and beginning work for this "better" paying company, you may end up with no job. Also better paying companies may demand more work, are stricter, and their fringe benefits may not be as good. So there is a lot to look for when shopping for and comparing jobs:

Type of work	Insurance (life, disability, medical, dental)
Number of hours (regular and overtime)	Bonuses
	Credit union
Work schedule (hours)	Car
Vacation and holidays (paid and how many)	Day care services
	Pension plan
Union	Cafeteria
Advancement	Profit sharing
Raises	Working conditions
Career goal	Fringe Benefits
Sickpay	Commuting cost and time

Do not quit your job before you have a new job. Do not make application for a new job until you have a strategy worked out. Be aware that your present employer will probably find out that you are looking for a new job, so think about how they will react when the news breaks.

Strategy

The first step in a career strategy is to evaluate yourself to see what qualities you have that are marketable, that you want to market. Doubtless, you are qualified for many types of jobs but try to find those qualities that you think you would like to employ in your work. The number of types of jobs is limitless. Just look in the newspaper want ads and you will see the great variety and diversity of opportunities. Realistically evaluate yourself under the following categories:

Education	Work experience
Personal skills	Financial
Physical condition	Ideal career
Interests and hobbies	

Thinking about the above will help you to organize the facts about your career strategy. A career strategy will not necessarily be a lifetime goal strategy. I include "Ideal career" as a consideration because you may want to take employment that will prepare you for your ideal career. In today's fast paced, rapidly changing world you may find that you will have several career changes over your lifetime.

After you have evaluated yourself in a realistic, almost coldblooded manner, you will want to take a long, hard look at the job market. Shop the job market. Pick a field where you want to work. Now make a resume:

Resume

Name
Address
Phone

Job Objectives
Education:
Name, location, relevant information (grades and major), and dates of attendance in last to first order.
Special activities at school
Work experience:
Name and location of employer and type of service performed.
Special skills:
Any you may have
Age   Service classification
Health   Citizen
References:
Name and address or available upon request
Method of reply
Thank you

Now that you have a resume you can consider ads for jobs and apply to companies you want to work for. When interviewing:
Be punctual
Be nicely groomed
Listen to what the interviewer says
Answer questions clearly
Ask questions about your job when the interviewer is done or as it may be appropriate.
Be honest

The biggest problems are:
Lack of grooming
Poor communication
Lack of strategy
Lack of interest

Start at the top when applying for a job. Who knows? Maybe you will get it. But don't waste your time if that job doesn't realistically look like it will pan out. Try another until you find a position that will be comfortable for you and your strategy. Try to work for a large company before going to a small company. Large companies provide the most training and the big name will carry you and impress prospective, future employers.

Be aware of your learning curve if you are planning to advance in your field. The learning curve is:

**AMOUNT YOU
CAN LEARN
FROM THIS
JOB**

1 Yr. 2 Yr. 3 Yr. 5 Yr.

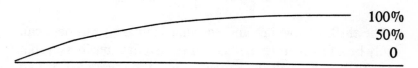

100%
50%
0

At the end of one year you have learned 25% of what you can learn from this job. By year 3 you have gained approximately 75-85%. After the third year it will take 2 or 3 years to learn the same amount you learned in year 1. A new job at this point (a strategic job) will put you at year 0 again where you will be expanding your horizons at a much higher rate.

Do not job-hop from employer to employer. A first job may be only one year if you feel that the job is just not for you, but your second job should be something you can stick with for longer and the third job longer yet. Employers in looking at track records place the most importance on strategy and reasons for changing jobs. Your employer is making an investment in you, you owe it to your employer to make the investment payoff.

Join a union where you work. It is right to collectively bargain for wages, fringes and working conditions. Unions usually provide medical and dental plans as well at a reasonable cost.

Join a professional association and be active. Trade

societies provide group insurance plans, literature, and meetings to keep you up to date on the latest and important news that affects you in your work. In addition to keeping you one step ahead of your competitor, organizations provide social activities.

Owning your Own Business

The thrill of owning and running your own business can really be a terror. Fifty percent of the average businesses that open their doors will close their doors in the first year or two of operation. The results can be financially disastrous and emotionally depressing. The reason:

Entrepreneurship

It takes a lot of skill and long hard hours to successfully begin a business. Just picking the type of business and location to operate is a major undertaking. Buying an existing business can be just as risky. After all, why would anyone sell such a successful operation?

If these hurdles do not scare you then begin your shopping. That is, you will have to learn a lot about operating a business. Go to the library, take a course at a local college in a small business, and I would especially recommend taking a course or at least reading a university level test on marketing.

When you think you have the knowledge and you still want to go ahead talk to a good CPA from a large firm and a real estate agent who specializes in commercial property. You will find that after having the proper marketing program and type of store, that the location and finances (money) of your

146

operation will be just as important. It takes all these skills working in harmony and a good deal of planning to make a reasonably good business operate successfully. Plan to carry the business for 6 months to get it off the ground.

Franchisors offer the same kind of opportunity to the potential entrepreneur. You should exercise extreme caution when dealing with these people as many times they will make their money regardless of whether you are making any money or not. Unscrupulous? YES! If you do decide to go with a franchise check it out with the Better Business Bureau and the City Attorney. Also try to pick a large well known firm. When you are ready to sign, take the literature and contact first a CPA who knows franchise operations to get his opinion and second to an attorney to be sure that your legal rights are protected, and you know exactly what the contract provides. Don't let anyone high pressure you or smooth talk you into anything that you have not personally checked out.

The same goes for other work at home or distributorship schemes. Give it a thorough check. If you are confused about anything the chances are that the scheme is a shaky operation. Skip it and report it to the BBB. There are enough legitimate opportunities available to get involved with anything else.

Divorce

Divorce is, of course, a very sad affair that I hope you do not encounter in your life. The statistics though are not all that encouraging. Your "odds" are worse, if you marry too young, have a small family income, low educational level, and live in the city. The finances of a divorce are disastrous to wife, husband, and children. Unless you are prepared to

147

halve your income you should reconsider divorcing (unless you live in a community property state). The law varies so much in each state that you should make it a point to find out what it is in your state. The library or a discussion with your family attorney will acquaint you with the facts that you should be aware of.

There are, however, certain facts about a divorce that are fairly uniform so I can discuss them with you.

1. In most states (except community property states) a typical divorce involving children may look like this:

Supporter	Supportee
40-60% of gross income	60-40% of gross income
½ savings	½ savings
pays lawyer fees	Children
	House (sometimes)
	Beneficiary of life insurance

2. If you hire an attorney to handle the case the fee will range from $100 to thousands of dollars. The cheapest way to complete a divorce is to make an agreement with your spouse that covers all the property and your rights without the aid of attorneys as arbitrators. Use your attorney minimally if at all possible. If the divorce goes well the only thing your attorney will do is draw up the papers and check out the agreement for its validity.

If things get tacky with squabbles try to estimate if your lawyers are getting more than you out of the squabble. It may be worth it but in most cases it will be easier to just agree and get it over with. Going as far as court to settle differences can be very expensive, not to mention traumatic. An out of court settlement, even if you must use a professional arbitrator or your lawyers, will be cheaper.

3. Happy hunting!

Wills

One of the most important documents you will or have signed in your life is your will. If you really want to give your relatives and loved ones a horrendous headache don't write a will. They will really love you dearly. Dying intestate, without a will means that the courts will have the job of dividing up your estate and responsibilities. The courts are often unable to make even a fair division of your estate since the law is very arbitrary in this regard.

By writing a will you will be able to have your wishes carried out just the way you would want to have it done. You can dispose of your estate in such a way as you see fit to those whom you want to have what you want them to have. If you have dependent children you will want to recommend someone as their guardian.

I do not here recommend how to make a will as you should definitely seek the advice of your attorney, but I will discuss those provisions that you should consider.

The first consideration is that you should not use a "form" to fill out your will. Everyone has different situations and a form-type may lead you to believe that it is all inclusive where it might not be. So you should take the time to have a professional document drawn up for you that will meet all your special requirements.

If you do not leave a will and the court does not recognize any legal heirs, your estate will revert to the state by "escheat". Escheat is the process whereby the state gains title to your property and then disposes of it.

If you have a large estate where there may be important tax considerations you should consult a financial planner. A financial planner will, in addition to getting your entire financial strategy together, be able to point out areas where planning will save considerable expense. For instance, naming the proper executor and considering the tax implications of your requests will expedite the matter at a most appropriate time.

The following sections are contained in a will:

1. The OPENING section tells who you are, that you are of sound mind, and revokes previous wills.

2. BURIAL explains how the expense will be paid.

3. Administration names:
   executor - who handles the disposition
   Trustee - administers any trust you set up.
   Guardian - who will take care of your dependents

4. DISPOSITION who is to receive what is described here.

5. SIGNATURE yours.

6. ATTESTATION - witnesses must sign

A will should be kept by your attorney or the executor. You should not leave it anywhere else. In addition to a will you will want to write a letter explaining:

1. Whom to notify in the event of death, including all relatives

2. Where all your important papers are including your Social Security card and life insurance papers.

3. Where you have pension plans.

4. What fraternal organizations or unions you belong to.

5. Where your safe deposit box key is.

6. The name and address of accountants, attorneys, financial planners.

7. A list of real estate, stock, other investments, trusts, and partnerships.

8. A list of important personal property including the location.

9. A list of creditors.

10. A list of savings and checking accounts.

Your will and letter should be able to orchestrate your final affairs.

If you are named executor of someone's will, you will have

to deal with the courts to settle the estate. This procedure is called probate. It takes at least six months to settle the affairs of any estate. If there is a will, the will is executed. If there is no will, the court will make the disposition of affairs. You might want two executors: One to handle the financial such as the trust department at your bank and someone in the family to handle more sensitive items closer to home. Be careful though in appointing executors as if there is more than one the fees may double. An executor is dismissed when all the following duties have been performed:

The will is put through probate in court which includes setting up the estate, collecting money due and paying money owed.

Managing the affairs of the deceased.

Disposing of all assests under the terms of the will, getting receipts for such and reporting all that to the court.

To avoid the delays of probate which can extend for a very long time especially if there is litigation and to keep costs down, property can be legally transferred without a will and probate through:

Life insurance, gifts, joint ownership, and trusts.

The complexities of gifts, estates, and trusts require a prudent person to consult a professional as to the best method of disposition. You should however, be aware that life insurance is not taxable and is payable without probate generally.

Changes in your will must be done in a specific manner to be sure that the change will be legal. Do not scratch out something and write in the change. You will have to draw up a codicil to properly make a change. A codicil is a formally drawn document that must be witnessed and generally comply with all the same rules for the writing of the original will. If you make a new will be sure that all copies of the old will are destroyed.

When would you want or need to change your will?

Check the following list:

A new executor
A new beneficiary
A change in the estate
A new residence in a different state
A change in the status of your beneficiaries.

You may have good reason to disinherit somebody but generally you cannot disinherit your spouse. The law will cause the spouse to receive ⅓ to ½ unless there are special circumstances. If one of your beneficiaries becomes wealthy you may want to disinherit the wealthy to give someone who could better use an inheritance. Give your reasons in your will.

Estates

Your estate consists of all the property you own and your responsibilities. The government has the right to tax your estate when you pass title to your beneficiaries in your will. Estate planning is setting up your estate so as to avoid taxes. Estate planning is an important step that should be considered before you write your will. If you do not plan properly your beneficiaries may not get what you want them to get. Taxes could force your beneficiaries to sell just what you want them to get in order to pay the estate or inheritance taxes.

If your estate is greater than $120,000 an estate tax return must be filed. Since gift taxes are less than estate taxes some of the burden of the estate tax may be lifted by making gifts. However, gifts made within three years of death are generally considered in the estate. You should most definitely seek the advice of your financial planner when contemplating your change in your estate.

Trusts

A trust is a legal agreement where you, the trustor give the trustee property to manage. When the trustee is done managing or during the term of the trust the property is dispersed to the beneficiary of the trust. You may be the beneficiary or anyone you name can be the beneficiary.

You may want to be the beneficiary if you put your stock in the hands of an investment manager whom you think can manage the funds better or easier than you. Most trusts set up a spouse or children as the beneficiary. The earnings of a trust may be used to do virtually anything that you instruct the trust to do. Inheritances are sometimes received in the form of a trust before death. Educations can be provided for under a trust.

A trust may be revocable or irrevocable. A revocable trust is one that you can stop at anytime. If you let a bank trust department manage your funds you will want a revocable trust. If the bank mismanages your money or you are not pleased with the service then you will want control. An irrevocable trust may not under normal circumstances be changed materially.

Funerals

The typical funeral will cost about $2,000. For this you get: transportation to the funeral home (local), embalming, your choice of caskets, use of a memorial room, hearse transportation to the cemetery, and free administration of life insurance and veteran's benefits, burial permits, and obituaries. If you join a memorial society for $10-$25 you will be entitled to have a pre-arranged funeral at a cost considerably less than the above ($400). A memorial society allows a dignified funeral at a reasonable expense.

If you do not join a memorial society you will want to get a full price quote from the funeral director. Not all caskets are always shown, some of the less expensive models may be in another location. Also it may be possible to view the deceased during the funeral in an expensive nice looking coffin and have the burial in a more practically priced one. The list of charges is below. Not all are incurred at the funeral home.

Funeral home
Internment recepticle (varies by cemetery)
newspaper notice
clergyman
gravesite
opening and closing grave
monument
sales tax

Cremations are arranged by memorial societies and funeral homes. A cremation may be immediate or with a viewing. The price for an immediate cremation is much less than with a viewing. A viewing involves a funeral service which may be before or after the cremation and scattering of the ashes in a garden. If you want the ashes scattered somewhere else check with the funeral director for state and local regulations. Some firms will want to have the cremation in an expensive casket which is totally unnecessary. A simple pine box is perfectly appropriate.

Veterans and social security recipients are allowed $250 and $225 respectively for funeral costs. You or your funeral director have to apply to receive these benefits.

Income Taxes

As Benjamin Franklin said there are only two things you can count on in life "death and taxes". The federal government, state governments, and if you are lucky your local government collect income taxes. Unless you are self employed your employer will withhold taxes from your paycheck. You must file an income tax form to get a refund if more has been withheld from your check than you owe, and vice-versa. Since the forms and law changes almost every year it is probably worthwhile to have a professional prepare your return. These people may be aware of sections in the code that can save you money. Most of us are able to prepare our own single returns but unless you go to an expert you may be wasting your time and money.

In order for your tax preparer to do a good job, you must keep good records. Your records should include-copies of your old returns, copies of your old W'2's

All income
Alimony
Annuities
Bad debt recoveries
Bonuses
Sales at a profit
Dividends
Interest
Gambling winnings
State tax refunds (if itemized)
Rents
Retirement pay
Royalties
Strike pay
Tuition paid by employer
Tips
Possible deductions
Not Itemized:
Bad debts
Business expenses (auto mileage)
Education
Business gifts
IRA contributions
Losses on sales
Worthless stock
Itemized
Accountant's fees
Alimony
Attorney's fees
Charitable contributions
Dues, union or professional

Education
Employment Agency fees
Casualty losses
Medical expenses
Dental expenses
Optometrist and glasses
Medical insurance premiums
Uniforms
Interest
Property taxes
Equipment used in business

You will need to keep receipts of these items. Also remember they are not all 100% deductible, some others are limited and have special rules.

If you are not sure whether you should file a return because of the amount of money you made or you can't pay what you owe you should file and pay. Sometimes the government gives "credits" to special groups in the form of refunds, even if you didn't make any money.

Self employed people should be especially careful to file a return that includes payment of Social Security tax that would normally be collected by your employer. You must pay this tax to get credit for Social Security benefits.

If you discover an error on your previous year's return you can file an amended return to correct the problem. Always double check your arithmetic and tax calculation. The easiest way to get an audit is to make an arithmetic error.

Keep your old returns, W-2's and receipts safely filed away

for at least four years, and longer if you have filed a particularly complicated return.

Retirement - Thinking Ahead

To many of us, retirement is a fuzzy cloud lying so far away that it seems like its hardly worthwhile to consider. To others of us it may be just around the corner or it may be something we are dealing with today. In any event it is a reality that will take up a significant time in your life. Making retirement an event that is pleasant is a job in and of itself. Just like shopping and investing, your money management policy will have significant effect upon the way you will be able to live your life in the golden years.

This will be a time when your social activities and recreation will be determined by the financial resources you have. If you retire in 10 years on a healthy 100% of the income you have now, you will be living at a little less than ½ your current living standard. To put it another way how would you like living now on your salary 10 years ago?

To determine how much you will need, take a look at your current budget. The basic and variable expenses you will have during retirement will be quite different. Savings and investments will generally no longer be in the budget as you will be living off the wisdom of your investments. In variable expenses furniture and education may be reduced the most and vacation and holidays increased the most. Children's expenses may be replaced by other dependent's expenses. Inflation will be a big factor in anticipating future needs. The table below may give you some idea of the power of inflation at 6% (compounded annually)

159

Years from today

	1	2	3	4	5	10	15	20
6% Inflation What costs $100 today will be:	106	112	119	126	134	179	240	320
8% Inflation Year: 0	1	2	3	4	5	10	15	20
100	108	117	126	136	147	215	317	466
Inflation at 10%:								
100	110	121	133	146	161	259	418	672

Even if you retire with enough to live comfortably, your cost may increase over the next ten years.

There is a way to beat these cost increase in your overall budget!

1. Eliminate as many of the costs as you can. Start with the big expenses.

   a. Own your own home, preferably clear of any debt. Your rent can never go up.

   b. Own your own reliable transportation if you want to drive a car.

   c. If you plan big holiday make a special savings effort before you retire. Dipping into the general fund for special occasions may leave you unprepared to cover general expenses.

d. Buy up in advance of your retirement those items you plan to use during your retirement rather than waiting until you're living on your retirement budget.

2. The other way to beat the cost increases is to have increasing income.

   a. Social security benefits are tied to the Consumer Price Index so your Social Security benefits will go toward some of your inflation prone expenses.

   b. Part time jobs may provide some hedge against increases in expenses as well as a diversion.

   c. If you own your home you may be able to refinance it for some emergency cash. (Warning: If you refinance make sure the new payments will work out in your budget).

   d. If you have interest in real estate, increased rents will be able to provide some hedge against increasing costs.

   e. Stock dividends also increase though they may vary considerably.

Examine your sources of income to try to match income and expenses. Do this in the year of retirement and 10 and 20 years later.

Estimated Income

Variable Income:	Year of retirement 0-20
	1 - 2 - 3 - 4 - 5 - 10 - 20

Social Security
Veteran's benefits
Part time work
Real Estate
Dividends
Capital gains
Other
Fixed Incomes:
Pension(s)
Annuities
Life Insurance
Savings
Interest
Other
TOTAL INCOME

Now take your estimated expenses (some will have to be adjusted for inflation) and subtract them from your estimated income to see if your retirement budget balances.

Balancing the Retirement Budget

Year	1	2	3	4	5	10	20
Estimated Income							
less Estimated Expenses							
Excess or deficit							

You will probably have to make several adjustments when putting your estimates together and as the years go by, undoubtedly conditions will dictate further adjustment. You should look at your plans every few years to see if you should make any major adjustments and a thorough review should be made every 5 years to bring the plan up to date.

Pension Plans

An important part of your package is a pension plan that provides retirement income. You should know whether your employer covers you under a pension plan and many other "details" that may be very important to you when you retire. By law, your company must make available to you a pamphlet explaining how your pension plan works. The important points to check and compare are:

Eligibility - How you qualify to receive benefits.

Vesting - When your pension rights are vested you will always have a claim on the money contributed to your pension. Know how long you have to work to receive a partial and a full vesting.

Benefits - Know how much you will receive in 5 years, 10 years, if you quit, are laid off or fired, or take retirement at 60 or 65.

Your contributions are always fully vested. Only your employer's contributions take time to vest. Many pension plans accumulate funds even if you are disabled. Surviving spouses are eligible for at least 50% of the benefit amount if the payment is in the form of an annuity. It is possible to transfer your pension to a new employer within 60 days if it is agreeable with your new employer. The procedure is called a tax-free rollover.

Keogh and IRA Pension Plans

In an Individual Retirement Account (IRA) the amount you contribute is limited to 15% of your earnings or $1500 whichever is less. The amount you contribute is tax deductible without itemized deductions and interest or dividends earned on the funds are not taxed until you begin withdrawing during retirement.

Keogh plans work in much the same way except that only self employed persons are eligible to participate. The lesser of 15% of your earnings or $7500 per year may be deposited into a Keogh plan tax free as in an IRA. You can begin withdrawing at age 59½ under both plans. If you withdraw earlier you must pay a tax penalty unless you have a qualified disability.

If you want to take advantage of these tax deferred retirement plans you will want to talk to your accountant first to be sure it fits in with your program. Then investigate the plans that the various savings institutions and mutual funds offer.

Annuities

I briefly discussed annuities in the chapter on insurance and said that annuities form a good base of income in retirement years. Purchasing an annuity along with term insurance is probably the safest way to get good insurance protection and save for retirement. Now I will discuss some of the types of annuities available and the kind of income you can expect under each.

Annuities are purchased so that you can be sure to outlive

your principal. That is you pay $10,000 for a lifetime of income starting at a certain age. If you had invested your money you might be tempted to withdraw more than the earnings. Too much of this dipping into the principal will seriously reduce your income base!

A straight life annuity is the simplest form. It is as described above:

Cost $10,000
Income $85/month

For women with a longer life expectancy the amount is somewhat less. The important point is that you get uninterrupted income for your lifetime. Some annuities offer a minimum guaranteed return in the event the annuitant passes away before much money is returned.

An annuity that provides payments for a lifetime for both you and your spouse is called a joint life or survivorship annuity. This type of annuity pays a lower monthly income but it pays throughout the lifetime of both of you.

A variable annuity tries to fight inflation by varying the monthly income by the value of a group of stocks. Some are sold with a fixed income amount and a variable income amount. In any event a variable annuity is definitely a risky venture, especially when you will be depending on the income to live on and that income is dependent on a group of stocks that will vary in price from time to time. The cost of an annuity will vary by -

1. the income you will receive

165

2. your age
3. the type of annuity you select
4. your sex

You can purchase your annuity in a lump sum or with payments over a period of time. The dollar cost to you will be less if you use a plan that involves payments over time. Be sure to compare the cost of the type of plan you want with different companies. The companies may have different names for the same type of annuity and slight variations of the same type so be sure that you are comparing like with like.

Also variable annuities which are much like a mutual fund have a similar sales charge (load) that you will have to pay whether or not you pay in installments or in a lump sum. So long as you are investing in a mutual fund type income why not just go ahead and pick an income type mutual fund instead!

Planning for retirement is a big step. Those of you who do plan adequately will be satisfied and well, those that don't - maybe you will make it the way you want to. Take the time to investigate the available possibilities by reading and talking to others about retirement. The more people you talk to the more ideas you will have to work with to make your retirement years enjoyable.

Chapter Eight

GETTING HELP WHEN YOU NEED IT

You, the consumer, may at some time need to register a complaint and find out what your rights are in a particular situation. Here in this chapter you will find the resources and the methods that are available to help you avoid the gyps, frauds, and what-have-yous that even the most conscientious consumer may sometimes fall victim to. Hopefully after reading this book and being a dedicated, expert shopper, your problems will be few and far between.

Keep the receipts for what you buy in a special place. When you get a warranty card with a new product, fill out and send it in. Keep your record of the warranty and instructions. together so you can easily refer to them.

Many problems are the result of improper use of a product. Other problems result when proper maintenance of a product is ignored. To get the most for your money read and follow instructions for your product. Keep your mechanical products and other items that require care in good condition by servicing them when recommended. After all, why spend as much time shopping to find a bargain if after you have it, you let your dollars go by the wayside by not maintaining what you have.

Other problems arise when the wrong product is bought. For instance, if you buy a spark plug that does not meet the specifications of your car, you could very well have a real problem. Make sure that what you buy will do the job you intend it to do. If it's a very special item for one time or limited use consider renting the product.

Well let's assume that you were somehow dealt a real lemon. So now you want your money back or a replacement.

First of all consider how much time and energy you will have to spend to solve your complaint. If the item you bought cost less than a dollar, for instance, and you bought it at a store all the way across town where you rarely shop, the cost of gas just to get there may cost more than any satisfaction you might get from returning your purchase. Don't make a special trip unless you have to; just wait till the next time you are going by that particular store to make the return.

To make a successful return, approach a salesperson calmly and ask to see the manager indicating that you would like to return (or get credit for) your lemon. the salesperson may be able to handle it or you may have to talk to the manager. I find the best way to approach anyone is to simply say "I bought this lemon here about two weeks ago and now it doesn't work because...". the manager will ask you if you have your receipt, hopefully because this means you can make your exchange or get a credit slip for the amount of purchase plus tax. Getting cash back may be more difficult, but if you persist through the inevitable sales pitch you can usually get your money back.

Sometimes a manager will not see it your way, so it may be worthwhile to go to the owner or some higher official to get action. Again calmly explain the circumstances. If no action is forthcoming then explain how you will seek further aid for your cause from even higher ups in the company.

Write a letter detailing your experiences to company headquarters. Include names, store address, and dates. Follow it up in two-three weeks.

If you still believe in your gripe after the above and you have not received satisfaction it is time to bring in the big boys—the consumer protection agencies.

The two agencies that will perhaps provide the most help are the Better Business Bureau (BBB) and your local Call For Action group. (CFA)

The Better Business Bureau will contact the company on your behalf to make an attempt to negotiate the problem. The BBB cannot force anyone to do anything — it's just that their voice has more clout than an individual's and may, therefore, get you some action.

If you want real clout call Call For Action. This is a national organization of volunteers sponsored by broadcast organizations like your local TV station. If you have really received poor response to a legitimate gripe these people will help you out. And if they can't help you they will destroy the company that gyped you: Unsatisfactory handling of a customer's complaints may land the company and the embarrassing complaint on the six o'clock news!

Small Claims Court

When the above course of action does not get you satisfaction you may be able to find satisfaction in the courts.

The court you will want to try first is the small claims court. What is nice about this court is that the process is quick and easy. In most states the maximum limit on the amount you can sue for ranges mostly from $200 to $1,000 although a few allow claims as high as $5,000 to be litigated in their court. The court dates are set very soon after you apply, usually two to four weeks.

The best thing about taking your claim to small claims court is that you represent yourself. No attorney is needed. You probably wouldn't want one unless the claim was for a high enough amount to cover the cost of an attorney. When you get to court bring all the evidence you can and simply explain to the judge what your product is and why you should be allowed to get a refund or whatever you think is a reasonable settlement. Always be courteous to the judge; it helps.

Once you have won your case you will feel fantastic, but you still have to collect. The amount you are awarded in court is called the judgement amount. Most people will pay you right away. If they don't you may have to use other means to collect.

The sheriff can help you collect, usually for a fee. Other means are attaching property with a lien or attaching wages. Both of the latter require further court proceedings.

If you are sued in small claims court you will have to prove that you are not responsible for what happened. If you think you really are responsible try to settle before going to court. Get it in writing!!! If the amount of money is substantial or if you are afraid that you may have done something illegal, give your lawyer a call or make an appointment to discuss the matter. If you cannot afford a lawyer check with the local bar association for the names of organizations that provide low cost or free legal aid.

Your Lawyer

Your lawyer is someone you like and trust who you think can handle your legal affairs competently. You should have a lawyer before you need one. Shop for a lawyer; ask friends, business associates if they have a lawyer they use all the time who is good.

The Marindale-Hubbel directory is a list of lawyers in the United States. The directory also very conveniently rates lawyers for legal skills.

If it is too late and you don't already have a lawyer and you need one you will be forced to make some quick decisions. If you are suing, you should be able to find an attorney who will work on a contingency basis. That is, your attorney doesn't get paid unless the case is decided in your favor. They may charge 33% for such services but rarely will a good attorney take a case on such a basis if there is little chance of winning. If they do not take the case on that basis but only on a fee or hourly basis you may be fighting a losing battle. If you are suing and you think you have a winning case for sure, take it to a neutral attorney and ask his opinion on the case. If he says you will win for sure then you may want to retain an attorney on an hourly basis rather than by 33%. Still try to give your attorney an incentive to get more for you. You might offer a percentage over and above a certain settlement to you.

If you are not sure your attorney is doing a good job for you ask what is being done. It is also possible to consult another attorney about how your's is doing the job you are paying for. Just don't tell your present attorney what you are doing.

Generally to get the best legal service you should go to firm lawyers. A firm can afford to hire the best attorneys. Also a firm can offer specialists in a particular field of law if you encounter an unusual problem. Patronizing a particular firm will encourage your attorney to give you good service.

Free or low cost legal assistance is available at:
Legal Aid Society
Neighborhood Legal Service
Law Schools
Bar associations offer introductory one time ½ hour counseling at a low rate.

Warranties

Just because your new stereo record player carries a warranty does not mean that if it breaks down tomorrow that you will get it fixed for free. A warranty only covers what it says it covers. It might be parts only, only certain parts, for a very limited time, or worse, it might be written by someone who will not or cannot honor it. So if you are comparing products take the above into account. If two products seem about the same in price and quality, check the warranty to see how the manfacturer will back up the claims for having a superior product.

Also, just as important is where your product will be serviced. Servicing by a local dealer is definitely preferable to sending the product to the factory and having to wait. An implied warranty means that what you buy should work the way it is supposed to. If it doesn't; take it back.

Where to Get Information

Information gives us the knowledge necessary to make important decisions. The following is a brief list of the basic sources of information. These are innumerable government and private agencies and organizations dedicated to making information available to you the consumer. Take advantage of these services. After all it is you, the consumer, who ultimately decides the kind and quality of products and services that will be available through your decision to buy or not buy a particular product. That's the system.

Government

Check your United States Government, State, County, and city listings in the phone directly. If you cannot get very far this way call a Federal Insurance Information Center at the toll free number nearest you.

If you are dealing with a particular agency that is giving you problems that are not being solved call your local congressman's office and detail the problem to an aide. The aide will most likely be able to clear it up.

Local government red tape can sometimes be cut through the use of an ombudsman. An ombudsman is a consumer advocate who may be found through your Local Legal Aid Society or Neighborhood Legal Services center.

Here is a list of some of the various federal agencies:

Department of Agriculture:
Farmer's Home Administration
Food and Nutrition Service
Dept. of Commerce:
National Bureau of Standards
Dept. of Health, Education and Welfare:
Office of Consumer Affairs
Administration of Aging
Office of Child Development
Rehabilitation Services Administration
Alcohol, Drug Abuse, and Mental Health Administration
Social Security Administration
Dept. of Housing and urban Development:
Programs: Crime Insurance
             Community Development Block Grants
             Emergency Homeowners Relief
             Fair Housing and Equal Opportunity
             Flood Insurance
Dept. of the Interior:
Geologic Survey
National Park Service
Dept. of Justce:
Federal Bureau of Investigation (FBI)
Dept. of Labor:
Passports
Dept. of Transportation:
Office of Consumer Affairs
Dept. of Treasury:
Internal Revenue Service (IRS)
Customs
Savings Bonds
Civil Aeronautics Board
Office of the Consumer Advocate

Commission on Civil Rights—minority rights
Consumer Product Safety Commission—product safety
Energy Research and Development Admin.—new energy
Environmental Protection Agency—pollution control
Equal Employment Opportunity Commission—jobs
Federal Communications Commission—radio TV
Federal Energy Administration—energy
Federal Home Loan Bank Board—bank operation
Federal Maritime Commission—freight
Federal Power Commission—power plants,
Federal Reserve System
Fair Credit Reporting Act.
Federal Trade Commission—antitrust
General Services Administration
Consumer Information Center
Federal Information Centers
Government Printing Office
You name it—they have it
Library of Congress
Pension Benefit Guarantee Corporation—pensions
Securities and Exchange Commission—stocks etc.
Small Business Admin.—loan and information
Veteran's Administration—medical, loans, veteran's benefits
Equal Opportunity: National Association for the
                    Advancement of Colored People
                    (NAACP)
                    1790 Broadway
                    New York, NY 10019
                    American Civil Liberties Union
                    22 East Fortieth St.
                    New York, NY 10016
Government: Consumer Information (Index)
             Pueblo, CO 81009

Insurance:	American Institute for Economic Research (life)
	Great Barrington, MA 01230
	Insurance Information Institute (Auto)
	110 William St.
	New York, NY 10038
Housing:	National Association of Realtors
	write or call your local board
	National Tenant's Organization
	425 13th St., NW
	Washington, DC 20004
Medical:	American Medical Association
	535 North Dearborn St.
	Chicago, IL 60610
	American Dental Association
	211 East Chicago
	Chicago, IL 60611
	American Hospital Association
	840 North Lake Shore Drive
	Chicago, IL 60611
	American Psychiatric Association
	1700 18th St., NW
	Washington, DC 20009
	Health Research Group
	7th Floor
	2000 "P" Street, NW
	Washington, DC 20036

Private Sources

Appliances: Major Appliances Consumer
Action Panel
20 North Waker Drive
Chicago, IL 60606
Autos—write the company headquarters or visit a dealer.
Counseling: Family Service Association of America
44 East Twenty-third Street `
New York, NY 10010
see American Medical Association
Credit: Associated Credit Bureaus
6767 Southwest Freeway
Houston, TX 77036
Environment: Environmental Defense Fund
162 Old Town Road
East Setauket, NY 11733
Natural Resources Defense Council, Inc.
15 West Forty-fourth Street
New York, NY 10036
Center for Science in the Public Interest
1779 Church St., NW
Washington, DC 20036
Environmental Action, Inc.
1346 Connecticut Avenue NW
Washington, DC 20036
Friends of the Earth
529 Commercial St.
San Francisco, CA 94111

Bankruptcy

Nobody wants to go bankrupt. It is the ultimate of all

headaches one could possibly get. When creditors are banging on your door and you are hopelessly lost in a debt so huge you cannot see a way out—consider going bankrupt.

Bankruptcy is a legal procedure whereby some of your debts may be excused. However, not all debts are excused and all your assets except those legally protected by statute may be used to satisfy creditors.

A Chapter 13 bankruptcy allows the debtor relief from creditors. The Wage Earner Plan as it is also known allows you to pay off everything in installments.

See your lawyer if you feel that bankruptcy is the answer. Your lawyer will be able to plan your bankruptcy so that you will come out in good shape. Certain assets that may be claimed by creditors may be converted into exempt assets.

Once you claim bankruptcy you may not do so again for six years.

After you clear your debts, prospective creditors will seek your money again as they know what debts you have. Also they have six years to collect. When or if you get to this point please reread this book especially the chapter regarding intelligent use of credit.

Contracts

A contract is legally binding AGREEMENT between you and someone else. The key word here is agreement. In order for you to agree to the terms of a contract presented to you, you must understand:

1. What is in it for you?

2. What you have to do to get it.

When negotiating a contract you should be clear on all the terms and conditions contained in the contract.

Contracts involving money should specifically and clearly state:

1. The Annual Percentage Rate

2. Monthly payment

3. Cost of the item

4. Total cost including interest and finance charge

Always insist that verbal agreements or promises made while discussing the contract are written into the contract.

When you buy a new house in a tract or use your existing house as collateral for a loan you are allowed a three day cooling off period to cancel the contract.

If you do not understand a contract, are confused, or feel pressured do not sign.

Wait until you can get someone who can properly interpret the contract to read it *and* explain it to you, preferably your attorney.

Deal only with reputable, well known firms when considering a contract. Check with the Better Business Bureau and the local trade association for reputation.

You do not have to pay on a contract that has been transferred to someone else to collect if your purchase was a fraud. Contact your local consumer protection agency.

If you are writing a contract give your lawyer a call to make sure your rights are protected and everything is legal. Illegal contracts are voidable.

Buyer, you, beware when making a purchase.